UNDERSTANDING
ANNE TYLER

Understanding Contemporary
American Literature

Matthew J. Bruccoli, *Editor*

UNDERSTANDING
Anne
TYLER

by ALICE HALL PETRY

UNIVERSITY OF SOUTH CAROLINA PRESS

For
Tierney and Courtenay,
Matthew and Ty

Copyright © University of South Carolina 1990

Published in Columbia, South Carolina, by the
University of South Carolina Press

Manufactured in the United States of America

Library of Congress Cataloging-in-Publication Data

Petry, Alice Hall, 1951–
    Understanding Anne Tyler / by Alice Hall Petry.
        p.   cm.—(Understanding contemporary American literature)
    Includes bibliographical references (p.   ).
    Includes index.
    ISBN 0-87249-716-X
    1. Tyler, Anne—Criticism and interpretation.   I. Title.
II. Series.
PS3570.Y45Z83   1990   90-12534
813'.54—dc20   CIP

CONTENTS

EDITOR'S PREFACE

Understanding Contemporary American Literature has been planned as a series of guides or companions for students as well as good nonacademic readers. The editor and publisher perceive a need for these volumes because much of the influential contemporary literature makes special demands. Uninitiated readers encounter difficulty in approaching works that depart from the traditional forms and techniques of prose and poetry. Literature relies on conventions, but the conventions keep evolving; new writers form their own conventions—which in time may become familiar. Put simply, *UCAL* provides instruction in how to read certain contemporary writers—identifying and explicating their material, themes, use of language, point of view, structures, symbolism, and responses to experience.

The word *understanding* in the series title was deliberately chosen. Many willing readers lack an adequate understanding of how contemporary literature works; that is, what the author is attempting to express and the means by which it is conveyed. Although the criticism and analysis in the series have been aimed at a level of general accessibility, these introductory volumes are meant to be applied in conjunction with the works they cover. Thus they do not provide a substitute for the works and authors they introduce, but rather prepare the reader for more profitable literary experiences.

M. J. B.

ACKNOWLEDGMENTS

For their assistance with my research, I wish to thank the staffs of the Rockefeller Library at Brown University, the Phillips Memorial Library at Providence College, and the William R. Perkins Library at Duke University, especially J. Samuel Hammond, Head of the Department of Rare Books. I am particularly grateful to Anne Tyler herself, who answered my many questions so very patiently.

Kind permission was granted by Alfred A. Knopf, Inc., to quote from Tyler's novels.

TEXTUAL NOTE

In most instances, two sets of page numbers are provided for each quote. The first numbers are keyed to the readily available Berkley paperback editions of Tyler's novels. The second numbers, in italics, are keyed to the original hardcover editions published by Alfred A. Knopf. (When pagination is identical, only one page number is provided.) Where there are minor discrepancies between the two texts, the quotations are taken from the hardcover editions.

CHAPTER ONE

UNDERSTANDING
ANNE TYLER

Understanding Anne Tyler

Anne Tyler is something of an anomaly in contemporary American literature. Though she has been publishing well-received novels for a quarter of a century, Tyler has been largely overlooked by the scholarly community. No books and only a handful of essays about her work have been produced in an era noted for the vigorous critical scrutiny of even quite minor writers. Further, though she has written eleven novels, it was not until the past two years, with the 1988 release of the motion picture version of *The Accidental Tourist* and the 1989 awarding of the Pulitzer Prize for Fiction to *Breathing Lessons*, that Tyler's name has come to be recognized by a public beyond her small but enthusiastic coterie of followers. And though she is classified consistently as a Southern writer, Tyler was born far from the South, a latecomer and an outsider in a region that, more than anywhere else in America, puts great stock in the importance of multiple generations of local experience and identity.

UNDERSTANDING ANNE TYLER

Career

Tyler was born in Minneapolis, Minnesota, on 25 October 1941. Her parents, social worker and journalist Phyllis Mahon and chemist Lloyd Parry Tyler, actively encouraged the creativity and intellectual pursuits of Tyler and her younger brothers. They also tried to live according to Quaker ideals, establishing themselves in a series of experimental utopian communities, including one at Celo, North Carolina, before settling finally in Raleigh, North Carolina, when Tyler was eleven years old. Though adjustment to this non-communal life was difficult—"I had never used a telephone and could strike a match on the soles of my bare feet"[1]—Tyler eventually entered fully into the life of the region. She did field labor on area tobacco plantations, listening to her coworkers' stories and absorbing the nuances of their dialect, the kinds of experiences that were essential to someone who had been writing fiction since early childhood.[2] She also took classes in the fine arts, with the intention of becoming a professional book illustrator. At Broughton High School she was fortunate to have as her English instructor Phyllis Peacock, who also had taught novelist Reynolds Price. The Price connection continued at Duke University where, on full scholarship, Tyler took his writing courses.

She did not major in English at Duke, however. Tyler's field was Russian, and after graduating Phi Beta Kappa in 1961, she did graduate work at Columbia Uni-

CAREER

versity (1961–62). Much of her early career was devoted
to librarianship. She worked as a Russian bibliographer
at Duke (1962–63) and then married Iranian medical stu-
dent and novelist Taghi Mohammad Modarressi in May
1963. As he did his residency at McGill University in
Montreal, Tyler worked as the assistant to the librarian
of McGill's Law Library (1964–65). At this juncture, after
years of feeling "no real sense of urgency or commitment" to pursue a career in writing,[3] Tyler began to
produce novels, most of which were praised not for
their literary value but for the youth of their author.
Walter Sullivan, for example, termed *If Morning Ever
Comes* "more than a respectable beginning for an
author who is just barely old enough to vote," while
Haskel Frankel, writing of *The Tin Can Tree*, remarked
that "it is unfair to harp on the lady's age but difficult
to ignore it. You read and you wonder. On page after
page she offers proof of a maturity, a compassion and
understanding one would expect to find only in a more
seasoned heart than hers could possibly be."[4]

Tyler herself seems not to have been affected by the
frequently condescending reviews of her earlier novels;
indeed, she seems already to have begun at this point
her lifelong policy of never reading reviews of her work,
as "I don't want to know how often I've missed connect-
ing."[5] Instead, she channeled her energies into juggling
her writing and her growing commitments to her family. As is evident from her essay "Still Just Writing" and
statements made to Wendy Lamb and Marguerite

Michaels, Tyler frequently found it difficult to be a professional writer as well as a full-time homemaker and mother to her two daughters, Tezh (born 1965) and Mitra (born 1967). The strain perhaps shows in her series of aborted novels. One such effort, still unpublished, was written before *If Morning Ever Comes*. Another, entitled *Winter Birds, Winter Apples*, was written after her second published book, *The Tin Can Tree*. Its manuscript is now with Tyler's papers at the Duke University Library. She also began work on a novel that proved to be so poor that she "threw [it] away after two or three chapters." Yet another book, *Pantaleo*, was completed but never published. It was the product of the difficult years between *Earthly Possessions* and *Morgan's Passing* (See Chapters Three and Seven). Eventually, however, Tyler managed to establish a work schedule that accommodated school hours and vacations, and despite its strictures she has managed to produce a quality novel every two or three years for twenty-five years. And though not until *The Accidental Tourist* and *Breathing Lessons* had she produced solid sellers (the first printing for her last novel was 175,000 hardcover copies), Tyler has nonetheless enjoyed increasing recognition.

That recognition had begun while Tyler was still an undergraduate at Duke, where she twice won the Anne Flexner Award for creative writing. More national recognition came with the *Mademoiselle* award for writing in 1966. In May 1977, Tyler was cited by the American Academy and Institute of Arts and Letters for her

OVERVIEW

past achievements and the promise of excellent work in the future, and that promise was quickly fulfilled. Her novel *Morgan's Passing* (1980) was nominated for a National Book Critics Circle fiction award and for an American Book Award. It received the Janet Heidinger Kafka Prize for fiction by an American woman. Her book *Dinner at the Homesick Restaurant* (1982) earned a nomination for a Pulitzer Prize for Fiction, and received the P.E.N./Faulkner Award. *Breathing Lessons* (1988), received the Pulitzer Prize for Fiction. With her daughters now grown, Tyler continues to live with her husband in Baltimore, where she writes short stories and book reviews in addition to novels. Currently she is well into the first draft of her twelfth novel, about a 17-year-old boy. An intensely private individual, Anne Tyler avoids public appearances and grants few interviews, which are always conducted by mail.

Overview

Not surprisingly, most of the little critical attention that has been directed towards Tyler has consisted of efforts to fit her work into traditional literary classifications. She has been variously termed a realist, a romantic, a Victorian, a postmodernist, a minimalist, a sentimentalist, a feminist, a non-feminist, and a naturalist—terms which generally are mutually exclusive, or at least stridently incompatible.[6] This confusion is

UNDERSTANDING ANNE TYLER

hardly assuaged by concomitant efforts to identify Tyler's literary forebears and contemporary cousins. Her eccentric characters and tragicomic world view have led several commentators to place her within the school of Charles Dickens—a reasonable connection to make, though Tyler herself maintains that she is hardly a devotee: "Dickens isn't someone I've read much of— *Great Expectations* while a daughter was reading it in high school is the only title that comes to mind. I write about those off-beat characters and that blend of laughter and tears because in my experience, that's what real life consists of." Other commentators place her in the intensely modern, angst-ridden school of such contemporary writers as John Irving, John Cheever, and John Updike, though she herself is inclined to disagree: "I think John Irving is a skillful writer, but I disliked *Garp* and would never model a character after T. S. Garp. (Or after anyone in *any* book, for that matter.) And since I don't see any similarity between my writing and John Irving's, I don't think either one of us has influenced the other." It would appear, indeed, that Tyler's true literary forebears, the figures within whose tradition she seems most clearly to be working, are the writers of the Concord circle, the great Russian playwrights and novelists of the nineteenth century, and the writers of the modern South.

One would do well to keep copies of Emerson, Thoreau, and Hawthorne on hand when reading Tyler's novels. She is deeply interested, after all, in the nur-

OVERVIEW

turance of the self (and especially a mature sense of self-reliance) and in the often contrary connections between self and family, and self and community. Her novel *The Clock Winder*, for example, explores how a young woman's interactions with the Emerson family reveal her—and their—often-unsuccessful efforts to determine the needs of the self and the precise nature of self-reliance in the contemporary world. Likewise, in books like *A Slipping-Down Life*, *Celestial Navigation*, *Searching for Caleb*, *Earthly Possessions*, *Morgan's Passing*, and *The Accidental Tourist*, Tyler returns to the Thoreauvian question of what the individual truly needs to survive. As her characters accumulate and discard furniture, clothes, baby supplies, relatives, and even modes of thought, Tyler reveals the tensions inherent in modern man's contrary urges to amass and to minimalize. Thoreau's call for simplicity resonates throughout Tyler's novels, as characters repeatedly seek to strip down their existences by abandoning belongings, running away, or, more maturely, by living deliberately, often in tiny apartments or trailers.

Nathaniel Hawthorne seems also to be an important Tyler precursor. Robert McPhillips made a tentative suggestion in this direction in his 1988 review of *Breathing Lessons*, arguing that Tyler's fiction "belongs to the tradition of the American romance pioneered by Hawthorne far more than to that of the realistic or naturalistic novel."[7] To be sure, the stylistic qualities that have come to be associated with Hawthorne—including the

UNDERSTANDING ANNE TYLER

slightly fey quality of *The Marble Faun* or the use of outsiders like Miles Coverdale to observe and comment
upon others in *The Blithedale Romance*—are strong elements in Tyler's work. But so too are other Hawthornesque elements. For example, many of her novels—
most dramatically *Earthly Possessions, Dinner at the Homesick Restaurant, Searching for Caleb, The Accidental Tourist,*
and *Breathing Lessons*—read very much like Hawthornesque allegories, with characters transparently representing particular moral stances or possible modes of
action. As another instance, Tyler is concerned with the
burden of the past, be it personal, familial, or (less com-
monly) historical. Macon Leary can barely function a
full year after his son's death (*The Accidental Tourist*); the
legacy of Justin Montague Peck hangs like a pall over
generations of his descendants (*Searching for Caleb*);
Charlotte Emory seeks to run away from the oppressive
weight of her childhood home, as much as from her
uncomprehending, guilt-ridden husband (*Earthly Possessions*); and Ezra, Jenny, and Cody Tull continue to suffer from their unsettling childhoods long after they have
reached maturity (*Dinner at the Homesick Restaurant*). Not
surprisingly, the burden of the past often leads Tyler's
characters to abandon the physical homes of their
youth, to yearn, like Jeremy Pauling, to move to a spare
cubicle in the desert or at the very least to put a sturdy
lock on the door (*Celestial Navigation*). As is evident from
Tyler's frequent habit of equating a house with the family that lives within it, she could appreciate fully what

OVERVIEW

Hepzibah and Clifford Pyncheon suffer in *The House of the Seven Gables*. Tyler herself disavows any kind of indebtedness to writers like Hawthorne, Thoreau, and Emerson—"I'm not conscious of 19th-century influences, nor am I fond of 19th-century writers." It seems possible, however, that these influences may be traced to Tyler's having been raised according to her father's "Emersonian ideal."[8] Literary influence can be most powerful when it is least conscious.

Tyler's apparent indebtedness to Russian writers is perhaps less surprising. On the most obvious level, many of her characters speak of Russian authors: the senior Merediths chastise Leon for reading "Communist" authors like Tolstoy (*Morgan's Passing*); Duncan Peck of *Searching for Caleb* immerses himself in Dostoevsky, "because I think he's a writer that impassioned adolescents . . . feel particularly drawn to"; Maggie Moran of *Breathing Lessons* attempts to read Dostoevsky, a writer Tyler chose because of his "long, hard book[s]." But more important than these references are Tyler's use of themes, techniques, and character types drawn from the Russian masters, though she herself maintains that there are limits to this indebtedness. Benjamin DeMott in a fine review of *Dinner at the Homesick Restaurant*, for example, observed that "there's a touch of Dostoyevsky's 'Idiot' in Ezra, a hint of the unposturing selflessness whose effect on people denied faith in the possibility of human purity is invariably to intensify cynicism"[9]—but Tyler remarks that "I can say for sure that I've never created a Dostoevskian character." Similarly, Paul Binding argues that, like Tyler, both Chekhov and Turgenev "present, in shapely works of fiction, a large gallery of related persons who define themselves in part through these diverse relationships," while Martin Levin in 1972 pointed out that Tyler "fills her pages with . . . richly-idiosyncratic characters who amble about in Chekhovian fashion."[10] The eccentric characters who populate Tyler's world would certainly seem to owe far more to the example of Chekhov than Dickens, while Tyler's much-discussed use (or misuse) of language—skewed dialogue, non sequiturs, illogical trains of thought—would be instantly familiar to anyone who had just read *The Cherry Orchard*. Tyler herself admits that "I did so much admire Chekhov during my college days that I many very well unconsciously echo him." Though Tyler confesses that she no longer aspires to be "another Tolstoy,"[11] she nonetheless puts to excellent use her extensive knowledge of Russian literature, and especially Chekhov.

The body of writing that has been most frequently associated with Tyler is, however, Southern literature. As the "Note About the Author" in the Berkley paperback editions of her novels attests, Tyler "considers herself a Southerner"; and though she harbors serious doubts about that statement,[12] she nonetheless has been frank about her indebtedness to some Southern writers, especially Eudora Welty. As she recalls in her

OVERVIEW

essay "Still Just Writing," Tyler had discovered in her high school library a book of Welty's short stories:

She was writing about Edna Earle [of "The Wide Net"], who was so slow-witted she could sit all day just pondering how the tail of the *C* got through the loop of the *L* on the Coca-Cola sign. Why, I knew Edna Earle. You mean you could *write* about such people? I have always meant to send Eudora Welty a thank-you note, but I imagine she would find it a little strange.[13]

To Welty, then, may be attributed Tyler's sense of authorization, her feeling that she could pursue a career devoted to recording in writing what she saw about her in the South. To Welty Tyler may also owe her keen eye for detail, her overriding interest in characterization, and "the ordering poles of her fiction: a sense of distance on the one hand and a gift of sympathy on the other."[14]

Then again, these qualities are likewise evident in two other Southern women writers with whom Tyler has been associated repeatedly: Flannery O'Connor and Carson McCullers. It is easy to overstate the O'Connor connection. Tyler's own impatience with organized religion and her usually scathing portraits of ministers remove her dramatically from the insistently Roman Catholic world of O'Connor, as does her careful avoidance of violence. There are no drownings or bull gorings

UNDERSTANDING ANNE TYLER

in Tyler's world, in which the very few acts of violence—Janie Rose's tractor accident (*The Tin Can Tree*), Timothy Emerson's suicide (*The Clock Winder*), Ethan Leary's murder in a Burger Bonanza (*The Accidental Tourist*)—either occur offstage before the opening of the novel or are passed over quickly. Further, Tyler is most comfortable with the world of the urban South, not the remote farms of most of O'Connor's characters, for whom the city is a kind of Hell. On the other hand, Tyler does share with O'Connor a tendency to use unlikely characters, like Jake Simms (*Earthly Possessions*) or Muriel Pritchett (*The Accidental Tourist*), as agents of revelation, though the epiphanies they engineer have nothing to do with God's grace and much to do with more accurate perceptions of the self.

Tyler's indebtedness to McCullers is more pronounced. They both write of characters who seem not quite to fit in their family circles, who yearn to run away, and who, more often than not, forge painfully a kind of compromise perspective that enables them to endure in a not-always-pleasant world. Perhaps more importantly, Tyler seems receptive to McCullers's dictum that we must learn to "connect" with one another, that love is one of the few defenses we have against a world that seems antagonistic towards a strong sense of both selfhood and freedom—existential ideas that become increasingly evident after *A Slipping-Down Life*.

The Southern writer who is mentioned most often in relation to Tyler is William Faulkner, although too

OVERVIEW

much has been made of the few parallels that exist between them. To be sure, *Dinner at the Homesick Restaurant* is, like *As I Lay Dying*, a deathbed novel using
multiple points of view; but Tyler has never read *As I
Lay Dying*, and in fact she does not seem to have a high
opinion of what little Faulkner she has read.[15] Certainly
the vast differences between Tyler and Faulkner would
tend to offset what little they seem to have in common.
For one thing, Tyler evinces slight interest in race: she
rarely uses black characters as anything but domestics
(the exception is Mr. Otis, in the digressive second part
of *Breathing Lessons*), largely because she feels ill-
equipped to address the black experience in America:
"I would feel presumptuous writing about black life as
if I really knew what it was like." Further, Tyler does
not share Faulkner's interest in the myriad Southern
speech patterns. Though early in her career she stressed
her interest in the richness of Southern dialects,[16] her
characters sound suspiciously like Northerners. Tyler
also lacks the Faulknerian interest in the ante-bellum
South (only *Searching for Caleb* ranges back to the nineteenth century), while she "doesn't share Faulkner's obsession with the South's perceived fall from an Edenic
state of grace, after the Civil War, perhaps simply because she was born in Minneapolis."[17] And though she
experiments with point of view in books like *Celestial
Navigation* and *Dinner at the Homesick Restaurant*, there
is nothing even remotely comparable to the experimentation of Faulkner's *Absalom, Absalom!* or *The Sound and*

the Fury. Indeed, her disinclination to experiment may be seen as a conscious reaction against Faulkner: "his whole approach to writing—obviously he was knitting off in all directions—was completely wrong for me. If it were possible to write like him, I wouldn't. I disagree with him. I want everyone to understand what I'm getting at."[18] And she certainly parts company with Faulkner in her apparent lack of interest in the matter of sexual activity—a lack for which she has been roundly criticized.[19] Tyler is quite defensive, however, on this score: "While I'm writing a novel I feel personally acquainted with my characters—almost in love with them, in fact—and responsible for the way they're presented. So I have never felt comfortable about exposing their sex lives. I believe I've been wrong about that in only one instance: *Celestial Navigation*. As I look back upon that book I see that it must be hard for readers to credit Jeremy with any sexual capability, and that I really owed it to them to show how he managed it. But Jeremy is the character I've felt most protective of, and so I let the book down on that account." But where Faulkner and Tyler seem very close is in their mutual insistence on one of the most important elements in human existence: the need to endure.

The world as Tyler perceives it is a decidedly messy affair. In addition to the burden of personal and familial pasts, her characters suffer from peer pressure (*A Slipping-Down Life*), child abuse (*Dinner at the Homesick Restaurant*), genetically-based predispositions (*Searching for*

OVERVIEW

Caleb), and poor self-image (*Morgan's Passing*). Most live in terror of the outside world, like Macon Leary compiling guidebooks to minimize contact with it (*The Accidental Tourist*) or Jeremy Pauling holing up in his studio in agoraphobic panic. Others try to escape but cannot, like Charlotte Emory, whose only successful departure is as the hostage of a befuddled bank robber (*Earthly Possessions*). Much of the apparent chaos in Tyler's fictional worlds is due to the fact that everything seems to happen as an incongruous blend of utter chance and utter doom: Jake Simms just happens to take Charlotte hostage, while Ethan Leary just happens to be in a fast-food restaurant when a teen-aged thug decides to murder all the customers; the Pecks seem destined from birth to buy only Fords and to despise plaids (*Searching for Caleb*), while Emily Meredith is destined to embark on a career in puppetry that seems genetically encoded (*Morgan's Passing*). The Tyler characters who do try to remain functional in this chaotic world rely on various strategies. One such strategy is the cultivation of ritualistic behavior, like the purchase of a new red toothbrush every winter (*If Morning Ever Comes*). Others try to create the illusion of control by assuming identities (Morgan Gower in *Morgan's Passing*) or acting more integrated than they really are (Elizabeth Abbott of *The Clock Winder*). Others immerse themselves in the world of games (especially Monopoly and solitaire), where the rules are clear and winning a real possibility. Others frantically demand to know "the point," be it the point of pursuing an unsuccessful music career (Drumstrings Casey in *A Slipping-Down Life*), of getting to class on time (Justine Mayhew Peck in *Searching for Caleb*), or of holding a funeral for a cremated husband (Serena Gill in *Breathing Lessons*). Others just as frantically try to blame someone, anyone, anything for all that happens, since blame implies an understood order and a feeling of control. Still others use a medium that is quite appealing to Tyler: the fine arts. Most notably in Janie Rose's "tin can tree" and Jeremy Pauling's "pieces" (*Celestial Navigation*), Tyler's characters try to integrate the seemingly antithetical fragments of the world, rendering incongruous images, ideas, and events into meaningful wholes over which they, as artists, exert control. Photography likewise is a frequent pursuit in Tyler's novels, as characters attempt to "freeze" particular moments, to save them from the exigencies of change, of passing time, and of seeming chaos.

In the course of writing her eleven novels, however, Tyler seems to have evolved a means of dealing with these exigencies that has little in common with rituals, role playing, or games. In their stead, her characters have come to rely on a strategy that exerts a measure of genuine, rather than illusory, control over their lives and the world. It is seen as early as *Searching for Caleb*, in which the fortune teller Madame Olita explains to Justine Peck that one of the most painful elements of man's existence, the weight of the past, need not be overwhelming: "you can always choose to *some*

OVERVIEW

extent. You can change your future a great deal. Also your past.... Not what's happened, no ... but what hold it has on you" (135, *129*). In a similar vein, Macon Leary of *The Accidental Tourist*, buffeted by the shocking death of his son and the dissolution of his twenty-year marriage, eventually comes to the realization that one may "choose what to lose" (301, *310*).

It is an upbeat stance, and one quite unusual for the contemporary American literary scene. No wonder she defies classification. Humanists like Anne Tyler are, after all, very rare indeed.

Notes

1. Anne Tyler, "Still Just Writing," in Janet Sternburg, ed., *The Writer on Her Work* (New York: Norton, 1980): 13.

2. As with most writers, Tyler began creating fiction at a very early age: "So far as I can remember, mostly I wrote first pages of stories about lucky, lucky girls who got to go West in covered wagons" (Laurie L. Brown, "Interviews with Seven Contemporary Writers," *Southern Quarterly* 21 [Summer 1983]: 11). With the move to Raleigh, Tyler began the process of establishing the geographic locale for her mature works. Though a few random scenes are set in such places as New York (*If Morning Ever Comes*), Florida (*Earthly Possessions*), Paris (*The Accidental Tourist*), and Pennsylvania (*Breathing Lessons*), Tyler clearly is most comfortable writing about North Carolina and Maryland, and especially Baltimore. It seems unlikely that future novels will be set elsewhere. As she explained to Bruce Cook, "I lived four years in Canada, and I could write practically nothing about it at

all" ("New Faces in Faulkner Country," *Saturday Review* 3 [4 September 1976]: 41).

3. Brown 4.

4. Walter Sullivan, "Worlds Past and Future: A Christian and Several from the South," *Sewanee Review* 73 (October–December 1965): 719; Haskel Frankel, "Closing a Family Wound," *Saturday Review* 48 (20 November 1965): 50.

5. Interview with Alice Hall Petry, conducted by mail in August 1989. Undocumented statements by Tyler are drawn from this interview.

6. Several commentators have remarked on Tyler's resistance to traditional literary classifications. For example, in his 1988 review of *Breathing Lessons*, Edward Hoagland observed that "though Ms. Tyler's spare, stripped writing style resembles that of the so-called minimalists (most of whom are her contemporaries), she is unlike them because of the depth of her affections and the utter absence from her work of a fashionable contempt for life" ("About Maggie, Who Tried Too Hard," *New York Times Book Review* [11 September 1988]:44). Similarly, Mary F. Robertson points out that "while Tyler would seem to be the last candidate for the ranks of the postmodernists, who are usually perceived as stylistically radical, her assault on the notion of what is a proper family makes her close in spirit to other postmodernists who regularly engage in what might be called category assassination, questioning just about every conventional distinction between one concept and another that we use to order our lives and thought" ("Anne Tyler: Medusa Points and Contact Points," in Catherine Rainwater and William J. Scheick, eds., *Contemporary American Women Writers: Narrative Strategies* [Lexington: UP of Kentucky, 1985]: 128). Equally unclear is the matter of whether Tyler is a feminist author, for although she does create strong women characters, such as Muriel Pritchett (*The Accidental Tourist*) and Justine Mayhew Peck (*Searching for Caleb*), she tends to place them in traditional roles as wives and mothers. In 1989, she reported that she does not care for novels written in the early 1970s by "the really strident, bitter, look-what-men-

OVERVIEW

have-done-to-us women writers who were popular at that particular moment. Certainly I don't hate liberated women as such; I assume I'm one myself, if you can call someone liberated who was never imprisoned" (Interview with AHP).

7. Robert McPhillips, "The Baltimore Chop," *The Nation* 247 (7 November 1988): 464.

8. The term "Emersonian ideal" is quoted by Anne R. Zahlan in her essay "Anne Tyler" in Joseph M. Flora and Robert Bain, eds., *Fifty Southern Writers After 1900: A Bio-Bibliographical Sourcebook* (Westport, Connecticut: Greenwood Press, 1987): 491.

9. Benjamin DeMott, "Funny, Wise and True," *New York Times Book Review* (14 March 1982): 14.

10. Paul Binding, "Anne Tyler," in *Separate Country: A Literary Journey Through the American South* (New York & London: Paddington Press, 1979): 204; Martin Levin, "New & Novel," *New York Times Book Review* (21 May 1972): 31.

11. Anne Tyler, "'Because I Want More Than One Life,'" *Washington Post* (15 August 1976), Sec. G: 7. In 1989, Tyler explained that "I love Tolstoy because of a single book, *Anna Karenina*, and that's for its fresh, subtle, surprisingly modern style" (Interview with AHP).

12. "I don't know why that blurb says I consider myself a Southerner. I don't, for one thing; also I am most definitely not a Southern *writer*, although I think of that as a very honorable tradition. Probably, way back when my first novel was published, the publishers stressed Minnesota in my biographical note and I pointed out that I was really more from North Carolina; but I can't be sure" (Interview with AHP).

13. Tyler, "Still Just Writing" 14.

14. Frank W. Shelton, "The Necessary Balance: Distance and Sympathy in the Novels of Anne Tyler," *Southern Review* 20 (Autumn 1984): 851. One must be careful, however, in trying to establish concrete echoes of Welty in Tyler's work. Robertson, for example, argues that Tyler "seems deliberately to invoke Eudora Welty's *The Golden Apples*" in *Dinner at the Homesick Restaurant:* "The connection becomes explicit when Beck Tull, who leaves his wife and children early in the

book, just as King McLain does in *The Golden Apples*, returns to Pearl's funeral—King returns to Katie Rainey's funeral; Tyler writes, "Kinglike, [Beck] sat alone" (124–25). Tyler revealed in 1989 that she never intended parallels between the two books: "No specific elements have been borrowed from [Welty's] work to my knowledge, and certainly not Beck's sitting 'king-like' [sic]" (Interview with AHP).

15. "To the best of my knowledge, I've never read *As I Lay Dying*. My experience of Faulkner came late in life—some ten or fifteen years ago I thought I ought to at least see what he was all about, and so I read a bunch of books about Snopeses, but they all ran together in my mind and I kept starting the same book over again thinking it was one I hadn't read, and then finding out I *had* read it (or maybe I hadn't but had read another one just like it . . .)" (Interview with AHP; Tyler's ellipsis).

16. In a revealing 1965 interview, Tyler explained that "I could sit all day and listen to the people talking. It would be hard to listen to a conversation in Raleigh for instance, and write it without putting in color. And they tell stories constantly! I love the poor white trash—they're fascinating and everything about them is so distinct. And I love the average Southern Negro—they speak a language all their own. A Southern conversation is pure metaphor and the lower you get in the class structure, the more it's true. Up North they speak in prose, and the conversation doesn't have as much color'" Jorie Lueloff, "Authoress Explains Why Women Dominate in South," *[Baton Rouge] Morning Advocate* [8 February 1965], Sec. A: 11). The only Tyler novels which seem to make use of distinct Southern dialects are *The Tin Can Tree*, published the same year as this interview, and *Breathing Lessons*, in which Maggie begins to mimic the black speech of Mr. Otis.

17. McPhillips 464. Though McPhillips's point is well-taken, it seems highly unlikely that Tyler's Minnesota birth had much to do with the matter.

18. Cook 40.

19. Edward Hoagland, for example, argues that Tyler "touches upon sex so lightly, compared with her graphic realism on other mat-

OVERVIEW

ters, that her total portrait of motivation is tilted out of balance" (44).
Vivian Gornick is even more emphatic, maintaining that "the energy
that ignites" people "is sexual in character, not filial." But "Tyler's
prose is sexually anesthetized—in fact, mass sexual coma prevails in
her books—and so the energy it gives off feels fabricated. The warmth
is shallow; it is nostalgia being burned, not immediate experience"
("Anne Tyler's Arrested Development," *The Village Voice* 27 [30 March
1982]: 41).

CHAPTER TWO

If Morning Ever Comes and *The Tin Can Tree*

Few writers profess much affection for their earliest publications. However, Anne Tyler's 1981 appraisal of her first two novels—"*The Tin Can Tree* [1965] and *If Morning Ever Comes* [1964] should be burned"—is more virulent than most.[1] Her statement hardly seems just: they are in fact interesting, highly readable novels, notable for sensitive characterizations (especially of children and the elderly) and for original, even poetic, images and turns of phrase. They also seem to have been structured with great care, a fact which would tend to belie Tyler's assertion that she dislikes her two earliest novels precisely because they are "formless and wandering."[2] But these two adjectives need not refer solely to novelistic structure; they also can refer to the establishment and development of themes, the accretion of appropriate and suggestive motifs and symbols, the careful rendering of dialogue—in short, the complex and often semiconscious art of selecting, developing, and molding one's fictional raw materials into a coherent whole, a meaningful vision that is aesthetically,

IF MORNING EVER COMES AND THE TIN CAN TREE

emotionally, and intellectually satisfying. To varying degrees, both novels do come up short in each of these areas; but even so, they stand as instructive introductions to Tyler's mind and art. For in *If Morning Ever Comes* and *The Tin Can Tree* one sees—albeit sometimes presented ambiguously, haltingly, or too insistently— four concerns that have come to be associated with the mature Anne Tyler: the dynamics of the individual and the family; man's inability or unwillingness to communicate; his responses, constructive or otherwise, to the exigencies of change and of passing time; and his quest for the patterns, and ultimately the meanings, underlying a world of seeming chaos. These four concerns, overlapping and mutually enriching, form the fabric of virtually every novel Tyler has written over the last twenty-five years.

Whether it is attributed to her Southern literary background or to her communal upbringing, from the outset of her career as a novelist Tyler has evinced a keen interest in the complicated relationship between the individual and the family. *If Morning Ever Comes* is in fact structured around a series of homecomings by various individuals from Sandhill, North Carolina: Ben Joe Hawkes returns home after four months at Columbia University Law School; his sister Joanne comes back after seven years of marriage in Kansas; his high school sweetheart, Shelley Domer, returns after seven years in Savannah; and Jamie Dower, age eighty-four, comes back for the first time after sixty-six years living and working in the Northeast. But none of these homecomings is pleasant, let alone triumphant. Old Mr. Dower, his son and grandchildren too busy to leave Connecticut, has come back to now-unfamiliar Sandhill in order to die in a nursing home that did not exist when he was growing up there. Shelley Domer has returned to live alone in a too-large, too-cold house, her sister and parents having died unexpectedly in a car accident. Joanne Hawkes has suddenly left her husband Gary and run back home with their infant daughter Carol, unsure of anything except her ability to attract men. And Ben Joe, who is pursuing a lucrative law career simply because "practicality was a good thing when you headed up a family of six women" (5), has bolted from New York without plan or purpose other than to confirm his status as head of the fatherless Hawkes household—a status which exists only in his own mind. As the reviewer for *Time* magazine pointed out, "The chill on Manhattan's Morningside Heights is nothing compared with that in the hearts of his family."[3]

The same pattern of negative interpersonal dynamics—the broken or ruptured family circle, the individual unwilling or unable to be part of that system—is evident in *The Tin Can Tree;* but in this second novel the situations seem more complex and intense because the homecomings are more psychological than physical. The most pivotal member of the novel's plot, six-year-old Janie Rose Pike, is never seen, having been killed in a tractor accident before the story opens. She "'kind of tipped everything over with her passing on'" (130, *131*), and it is the readjustment process—what Haskel Frankel terms "the closing of a family wound and the resumption of life among people stunned by the proof of mortality"[4]—that the novel traces. Janie Rose's parents, understandably distraught, find that process prolonged and difficult. Her mother "Lou," the best seamstress in Larksville, North Carolina, effectively ceases to function after the funeral, spending her days lying in bed and unwilling even to talk. Her father Roy sits all day, staring at the tree which little Janie Rose had decorated with tin cans and popcorn (since eaten by birds). Her ten-year-old brother Simon is distressed that her coffin is in the cold earth—the always-chilly Janie Rose "'had a twenty-pound comforter on her bed, middle of summer'" (10, *9*)—and that her aunt and uncle had sent gladioli, flowers she had hated because they look like "witches' wands" (131, *132*). The Pikes' extended family is likewise disrupted by the child's death. Simon's adult cousin Joan, who has been living with the Pikes for several years and who had liked to pretend that the two youngsters were her own children, impulsively decides to run back to her parents, then just as impulsively returns to care for Simon. And the Pikes' neighbor and close friend, photographer James Green, is reunited with his own family in a neighboring town after years of estrangement when he goes there in search of the runaway Simon.

But as with *If Morning Ever Comes,* none of these processes of family disruption and reconciliation is as tidy as one might expect. Mrs. Pike mourns her daughter not because she loved her—overweight and obnoxious, Janie Rose is hardly the "angel child" dying young and pure in so many nineteenth-century American novels—but because she feels guilty over having neglected her. Mr. Pike, although upset over the child's passing, is more frustrated by his inability to help his wife out of her depression, and he returns to work on a tobacco farm to escape her as much as to earn money. In contrast, their son Simon seems to handle his sister's death rather well: once he has been reassured that she is unaware of either the cold earth or the gladioli, he seems to be adjusting nicely, calmly eating his customary peanut butter and mayonnaise sandwiches. However, his recovery is seriously undermined by his mother's callous treatment of him, as she leaves him in the care of others and rejects the special photograph for which he had so happily posed.

Equally unable to cope is Joan Pike, who likewise lacks a loving, supportive family. Having been born to a couple well into middle age, Joan had always been treated like a visitor instead of a daughter. Emotionally crippled, she continues to feel like a guest wherever she goes, dutifully "hanging her towel and washcloth on a bar behind her [bedroom] door" (33, *32*) and never acquiring more than she can pack into two suitcases "with room to spare" (214, *216*). Her sudden decision not to

IF MORNING EVER COMES AND *THE TIN CAN TREE*

run away to her parents' home reflects feelings of exclusion and fear about her own family circle as much as love for little Simon. And James Green's homecoming is successful only in that he now sees that his father, a fundamentalist tyrant who had driven him from Caraway to Larksville years before, is in old age simply "a small, battered bird" yearning for his favorite rocking chair (249, 252). This modified perception does not, however, bode well for the future of the Green family: James attempts to warm his hands at the family fireplace—and then realizes that there is no fire. He returns to Larksville to continue his courtship of Joan, one presumably doomed by his unwillingness to marry her and create a new family circle of their own.

The large number of characters in both novels who are rejected or emotionally damaged by their own families would suggest that, in large measure, Tyler perceives families not as stable, nurturing entities but as potentially serious liabilities—and especially so for sensitive, independent, or, ironically, role-bound individuals. Janie Rose Pike, for example, sounds as if she had been a tough little cookie, setting fire to a field with her lit cigarette and scorning the dolls and "Little Miss Chubby" clothes that her mother had bought for her. But she clearly also had been a deeply sensitive child: a bedwetter, she suffered from brutal nightmares, refused to put dresses on over her head for fear of becoming invisible, became distraught over being served a "dead chicken" in lieu of a vegetarian meal (62), brushed her teeth "over and over with scalding hot water" when her pet hamster ran away (34, *33*), and wore layer upon layer of underclothes on her "bad days"—so much so that the straps of her overalls "would be strained to the breaking point" (39, *38*). The Pike family's tendency to ignore or to laugh at this sensitive child had left Janie Rose, at the age of six, a deeply troubled individual whose early death had probably spared her a lifetime of pain. Families are likewise liabilities for independent individuals. Ben Joe Hawkes, for example, acquired his bizarre habit of reading upside-down simply because his parents refused to acknowledge his natural impulse to begin reading at the age of three. Perhaps more dramatically, James Green sensed early on that his "tight little Church of God" father (208, *210*) was ruining the lives of his children. James began running away from home at the age of four—"'We locked doors and tied knots,' said Mr. Green, 'but he was like Houdini'" (255, *258*)—and expressed his anger at his father by rocking "fiercely" in the forbidden paternal chair when his parents went to evening Bible classes (249, *252*). That James's other independent sibling, sister Madge, went as far away from her parents as possible when they broke up her one romance (she became a missionary in China) would suggest that there is a broad spectrum of independent actions, and of responses to family strictures, at work in Tyler's novels—a spectrum full of subtle gradations that may explain James's strikingly ambivalent resolu-

IF MORNING EVER COMES AND *THE TIN CAN TREE*

tion to his own situation: he becomes a photographer who specializes in family portraits, and he continues to care lovingly for his brother Ansel in a town within easy driving distance of Caraway. That Ansel is a couch-bound hypochondriac—and that James, knowing Ansel is not really ill, seems actively to encourage his dependent behavior—suggests that his impulse towards independence from his family is countered with a desire for familial love, with guilt, and with an impulse towards self-abnegation. Understandably unable to sort out his own feelings about selfhood and family, James is unable to nurture his relationship with Joan.

James's complex situation suggests the power of the abstract notion of family and of the roles traditionally imposed within that context. That power is particularly evident in *If Morning Ever Comes*. Ben Joe Hawkes is visibly upset that his sisters, mother, grandmother, and niece neither need nor want him in their lives: "Why can't they all just let *me* take care of them?" (145) he moans to Shelley, as he recounts how they "forget" to write to him about important events in the Hawkes family circle. Ben Joe has difficulty accepting that the historical era has passed when he, as the sole male in the family upon the death of his physician-father, would automatically have become its de facto father figure: long gone are the days when Ben Joe, as a "Carolina white man," would necessarily be living in a particular kind of home, eating particular kinds of meals, and enjoying the deference of a particular kind of family (26). Demographic and socioeconomic changes have inverted that romantic, man-centered world. His mother and sisters have jobs and incomes, thereby making his pursuit of a law career a meaningless gesture. His state of mind over this is conveyed through his encounter with a game token on the living room floor: "His heel crushed something; it was the flatiron from the Monopoly set. He scraped it off his shoe and kept going" (161). The annoyance ("He scraped it off his shoe"), determination ("kept going"), and veiled violence ("crushed") implicit in this encounter suggest his painful awareness that the Hawkes women (flatiron) hold the power (Monopoly) in his family, a power based on "real" money: they support *him* at Columbia, sending him a check every month and expecting a receipt (14). No wonder Ben Joe cannot figure out how old he is: "He felt unsure of his age; in New York he was small and free and too young, and in Sandhill he was old and tied down and enormous" (34)—old from feeling compelled to play the role of a father figure to a family that had driven away the real father to die of a heart attack, unmourned and unmissed, at the home of a mistress. In the course of the novel Ben Joe comes to face, if not accept, that the role is an inappropriate one, and that the pursuit of it in an unreceptive family can only continue to exhaust him. So he will do the next best thing: he will marry family-less Shelley Domer and take her to New York, where they will live in presumed familial bliss with a baby boy. Ben Joe will get to be a father and a head of household after all, even if not as he had originally planned. Family roles do die hard.

The other element which renders families liabilities is one that will be developed much further in late novels such as *Dinner at the Homesick Restaurant:* the compulsion to repeat undesirable family action patterns. In *The Tin Can Tree*, those observing the situation are shocked that Mrs. Pike begins to reject young Simon in the same way she had rejected Janie Rose. One would expect that this bereaved mother would learn from her past mistakes, even lavish extra love on the surviving child to compensate for the neglect of the dead one. But instead she abdicates, leaving others to clothe, feed, and love her son until the crisis of his running away jolts her into being responsive to him once again. Likewise, in *If Morning Ever Comes* Joanne has left Gary after seven years of marriage out of terror that she, like her "cold-hearted" mother Ellen (63), was "making the house cold" for her young husband—that, in effect, "history was repeating itself" (239). Not until he visits her childhood home does Gary comprehend that Joanne was referring to the Hawkes family history. Tyler's handling of this motif is not effective in these two early novels. Mrs. Pike's neglect of Simon may be attributed to shock and grief rather than the resumption of a pattern of child neglect, while the resolution to the problem is too swift, complete, and contrived to be convincing. Similarly, the double metaphor of cold and warmth in *If Morning Ever Comes* is unoriginal and badly overused: it

UNDERSTANDING ANNE TYLER

is a bit much that "coldhearted" Ellen Hawkes is a Northerner, that her unfaithful husband died after going out for ice cubes, and that poor Ben Joe, rejected by his own family, desperately hugs a stray cat "to keep it warm" (154) while it wants only to be left alone.

All this is not to say that families, nuclear or extended, are uniformly negative in Tyler's first two novels. She acknowledges, for example, that they can be helpful in times of crisis. The Pikes survive the tragedy of Janie Rose's death thanks in large measure to the efforts of Joan, James Green, and others (such as talkative Connie Hammond) that these extended family members have called upon. Likewise, Joanne—significantly, her married surname is not given—can return to the Hawkes family fold in Sandhill while she and Gary work through their problems, secure in the knowledge that her old room is intact and that baby Carol will be well cared for as she seeks employment. Also, families can be an important source of identity. Though he dies alone in a Sandhill nursing home, old Mr. Dower— born "Algernon Hector James Dower the Third" (164)— derives comfort and pride from the knowledge that his was once the most powerful and respected family in town. Families also can be a significant source of a sense of continuity in an often confusing world. From baby Carol's true "Hawkes nose" (88) to the tiny pink sweater worn by generations of Hawkes girls, families provide a network of biological and material connections across time and space. However, each of these advantages has

IF MORNING EVER COMES AND *THE TIN CAN TREE*

a downside. Families may prove disconcertingly ineffectual in a crisis, even, as in the case of Mrs. Pike's rejection of Simon, making it worse than it need be. Or their
too-easy capacity to shelter their members from a difficult world may prevent psychic and emotional matura-
tion: had her husband Gary not suddenly appeared to
face their marital problems, Joanne conceivably would
have remained forever in her childhood home, ensconced in a bedroom full of "huge stuffed animals,
won by long-ago boy-friends at state fairs" (75). Or the
identities they impose may be inappropriate, even burdensome, or they may absorb individual identities
within the larger identity of the family itself: the
Hawkes sisters, after all, are barely distinguishable.[5] Or
the feelings of continuity and kinship they provide may
be conducive to emotional isolationism, although the
incestuous urges which some commentators have detected in *If Morning Ever Comes* are so subtle that Tyler
herself may not have been conscious of them.[6]

In the final analysis, families are ambivalent entities
in Tyler's novels, a matter conveyed rather transparently in these two early novels by the depiction of family dwellings. The Hawkes home, replete with stained
glass windows that "popped up in unexpected places"
and a turret that one expected to be "stuffed with bats
and cobwebs," looks very much like a haunted house—
an impression countered, however, by its front porch,
"big and square and friendly" (46). Upon entering the
house, one is confronted with a "mossy brown smell":

it "seemed to be part and parcel of the house and was a wonderful smell if you were glad to be home"—but "an unbearable smell if you were not" (46–47). These dualities (haunted/friendly; wonderful/unbearable) underscore how the same family can be a liability for Ben Joe but a source of considerable contentment for his sisters. Similarly, the isolated three-family house in *The Tin Can Tree* is perhaps too obvious an emblem of the interconnectedness of the story's three family circles: the Pikes, the Greens, and the elderly Potter sisters. No family can ignore or escape the problems within or without its walls. James literally can hear his neighbors snoring and crying out in their sleep, as the maternal spinster Miss Faye Potter, on perpetual night patrol, taps out inquiries and reassurances with her thimble. Both claustrophobic and comforting, the three-family house forces its seemingly marooned inhabitants, for better or worse, constantly to interact.

How one house, one family one be the best and worst factor in different individuals' lives is due largely to Tyler's second thematic concern: the limits of human beings' ability to communicate. At this early stage of her novelistic career, Tyler focuses primarily on oral and written communication; later novels will use more subtle and complex modes, such as body language and facial expression. Even so, Tyler probes the inadequacies of oral and written communication rather effectively in these two novels. Ben Joe Hawkes, for example, is never seen writing anything longer than a postcard; indeed, he plots to write a succession of them to his sister Susannah in lieu of a letter, hoping that she will infer from this barrage of missives what he is inexplicably afraid to state directly: that he would like her to mail to him in New York the prized possessions he had left in her care in Sandhill. Unlike the befuddled and evasive Ben Joe, his businesslike sister Jennifer writes long letters, signed "Sincerely" and postscripted "Enc." (14), selectively omitting vital information (such as Joanne's return home) that she does not wish him to know and attending carefully to the mundane financial aspects of maintaining an old house and a large family. More cogently, the apparently well-adjusted Jenny is capable of expressing herself openly, including her emotions: she is upset that Gram has taken to buying crabmeat and black olives for their Monday night casseroles, and says so. In contrast, Ben Joe cannot convey his feelings, especially on matters of more vital import. Indeed, he and Shelley, affianced on impulse ("We could . . . hell, get married" [209]), seem ideally suited precisely because they have difficulty expressing themselves, however "talky" (99) they may be on occasion. Here is their non-dialogue in the Sandhill train station as they elope to New York:

Ben Joe hunched forward and said, "What is it, Shelley? What've you got to tell me?"
    "I came by taxi," she said after a moment.
    "What?"

"I said, taxi. I came by taxi."
"Oh. Taxi."
He stood up, with his hands in his pockets. (259)

Most of the rest of their conversation is obliterated by the roar of the arriving train, the symbol that they are eloping due to a rush of events beyond their control rather than to love or reason.

Even more striking in these two early novels is Tyler's impulse to probe the limitations of even seemingly clear statements. In *The Tin Can Tree*, the elderly Potter sisters are taken aback when Mr. Pike asks them to try to talk to his mourning wife, bedridden upstairs: "You think you could just run up there a minute?" They demur: "Well, not *run*, no but—" (51). Likewise, Ben Joe in *If Morning Ever Comes* responds automatically to old Mr. Dower's announcement that he's come home to Sandhill to die: ". . . I trust that'll be a long time from now." Responds Mr. Dower: " 'Don't trust too hard' " (43). Time and again in these two novels, colloquialisms are taken literally, pleasant small talk generates friction, and set speech patterns are challenged openly. These are important sources of humor through irony, but they are more important as implied commentaries on the lack of thought or feeling underlying what generally passes for communication. When people do speak directly or pointedly, such as Ellen Hawkes's demand to know why her son Ben Joe is home from law school in the middle of the week, they sound oddly cold and distant.

IF MORNING EVER COMES AND *THE TIN CAN TREE*

Indeed, though Tyler never explains why Dr. Phillip Hawkes deserted his family and moved in with Lili Belle Mosely, this dowdy but warm mistress conveys the truth: "If your mother'd said one *word* he'd have stayed with her, always would have. He was just wanting her to ask him. But she didn't" (126). That their marriage hinged upon a single word suggests the power of words—and the power of silence. Ellen Hawkes's directness of speech coexists peacefully with her refusal to talk at all about deeply emotional matters, one of the few traits she shares with her son. When she learned of the birth of her husband's illegitimate baby, she "clamped her mouth shut and said that was *his* lookout" (117). The unexpected return home of her married daughter Joanne garners a similar response: "What's done is done, and it's none of our affair" (19). Of course, on one level these may be seen as intelligent responses to difficult situations. Dr. Hawkes probably suffered more from his wife's silence than he would have from a tirade, and Joanne does have to work out her own marital problems. But on another level, Ellen's silences may be seen as childish denials of reality, much in keeping with the family's refusal to discuss either Joanne's early near-elopement with a raincoat salesman or her compulsion, shortly thereafter, to play with "a new trick, a piece of plastic that looked just exactly like vomit" (191). These silences, plus Ben Joe's frantic elucidation of them and his family's negative reaction to his outburst (Joanne, for example, tries to choke him with

her coat), suggest that many of the difficulties in the
Hawkes family are attributable to a lack of basic communication skills. It is an important problem that Tyler will
explore at much greater length in her later novels, most
notably *Earthly Possessions, Dinner at the Homesick Restaurant*, and *Breathing Lessons*.

Rather less successful is Tyler's exploration of a different angle of the communication problem: the nature
of words themselves. They may be misheard and hence
misunderstood, as seen in Janie Rose's prayer "Deliver
us from measles" (31, 29). Also, words often are
freighted with emotions and potential prejudices: Ben
Joe's dislike of Joanne's husband, whom he had never
met, was based solely on his given name, Gary, which
reminded him "of a G.I. with a crew cut, and 'Mom'
tattooed on his chest, and lots of pin-up pictures on his
wall" (52). And words are so potentially powerful that
at times they seem to have physical substance. In *The
Tin Can Tree*, Joan Pike feels she is being "swept away
and drowned" by all the "useless words [of Ansel
Green] spilling around her" (81, 82), while Connie
Hammond, walking away from James at her family reunion, leaves a disembodied self behind: "the last part
of her to fade away was her voice" (68, 67). Not surprisingly, written words in these two novels likewise often
seem substantial. Long after segregated waiting rooms
have been abolished in the Sandhill train station, the
outlines of the words "white" and "colored" are still
eerily evident on the walls. No wonder James Green's

IF MORNING EVER COMES AND *THE TIN CAN TREE*

father is terrified of the telephone, "A *wavery* thing . . . On a thin line between what's real and what isn't" (251, 254). Tyler's is an *Alice in Wonderland* world in which words seem unreal, unreliable, unfixed, and even, at times, physically solid. It is an interesting and potentially rich motif; but it also is obvious and readily overused, and that poses a problem in these two early novels. The serious statements Tyler is trying to make are undercut too often by inappropriate word-based humor and by what seems to be semantic play as an end in itself. Tyler will never cease using language in this fashion, but she will utilize it in more subtle, appropriate, and hence effective ways in her later novels.

The "wonderland" aura of these two books—what Jonathan Yardley identifies as a "magical, slightly fey and otherworldly" quality[7]—is also attributable partly to Tyler's handling of her third major concern, the twin exigencies of change and of passing time. They are such prominent elements in the early Tyler that these first two novels seem to have almost slippery fictional landscapes where reality has become unmoored due to too much—or, paradoxically, to too little—change. The characters respond to these conditions by resorting to such strategies as running away, self-concealment, self-incarceration, denial, or combinations thereof which often are at cross-purposes and hence counterproductive. In *The Tin Can Tree*, for example, Joan Pike, overwhelmed by the familial turmoil engendered by Janie Rose's death (too much change) and the stalemate of her relationship with James Green (too little change), is visibly uncomfortable: she never "leaves" rooms, she always "escapes" from them (e.g., 49, *48*). Eventually she literally runs away, surreptitiously taking the bus back to her parents' home. But she is unable to follow through with this plan; she runs back to the Pikes and a kind of psychic stasis, having convinced herself that the displaced maternal love she feels for little Simon is ample compensation for a situation she finds otherwise intolerable. Other characters in this novel, including Simon and James Green, also resort to running away. But perhaps even more revealing are those characters who engage in literal or figurative self-concealment or self-incarceration. The gently comic Potter sisters, Miss Lucy and Miss Faye, have barricaded themselves within their third of the triplex house in Larksville. Without even a screen door to serve as a tentative link to the uncertain world outside, the Potters double-bolt themselves inside their home, which is honeycombed with "a labyrinth of tall black folding screens" that divides their living space "into a dozen or more tiny rooms" (115, *116*). It is an extreme and perhaps too transparent emblem of the novel-wide impulse to hide out from life, including Ansel's self-made prison of chronic hypochondria and Mrs. Pike's self-confinement in her cluttered bedroom. True, she is mourning Janie Rose, but she also is attempting to remove herself from that world of pain and change that took her daughter's life—a removal signified by her desire literally to stop all the

IF MORNING EVER COMES AND *THE TIN CAN TREE*

clocks in her home, to prevent the change-generating movement of time itself.

Mrs. Pike's terror of change and time in *The Tin Can Tree* is shared by Ben Joe Hawkes in the earlier novel, although Tyler's treatment of his case is more subtle and provocative than that of Mrs. Pike. The very title of *If Morning Ever Comes* suggests a waiting for change that will come only with the passage of time,[8] but its very tenuousness ("if," "ever"—not "when") underscores Ben Joe's frustration and even ambivalence about change as it will affect him personally. This pattern seems to have been long-term. As a youth he essentially had been a helpless pawn in his parents' marital struggles, going to Sandhill College (minor change) instead of Harvard (major change) only because his mother refused to let her estranged husband use the money he had saved so carefully for his son's education. Thus graduating from high school, an important change coming at a key time in one's life, had been for Ben Joe a monumental disappointment which demonstrated his lack of control over his own existence. After graduating from college, he did virtually nothing for several years, effectively cutting himself off from change and time by hiding out in Sandhill. At twenty-five he began law school at Columbia. As the story opens he is avoiding classes, preferring to conceal himself in the tiny apartment which he shares with an undergraduate far more mature than he, and cocooning himself in a "crazy quilt from home" (6). After just four months at Columbia he

UNDERSTANDING ANNE TYLER

impulsively runs back to Sandhill, an act which seems initially to denote major change but which in fact denotes a desire to nestle in a stable, changeless, timeless world where he, as a male, will have a ready-made, prominent niche. What he finds, of course, is that the antebellum world is long gone and that the protofeminist movement of the 1960s has obliterated whatever remnants of it may have been enjoyed by Ben Joe. So he responds in the only way possible: he impulsively proposes to Shelley. Once again, what looks like a major change (marriage) is actually an attempt to contain or prevent change: like something out of a time warp, Shelly is "a remnant of his youth,"[9] a girlfriend from the seemingly timeless long-ago of high school rather than the confusing present; she will know her place in a traditional marriage, one based on what she has read in those "homemaking magazines" (265); and their new apartment will be "like his own little piece of Sandhill transplanted" (265)—including, presumably, that other comfortingly familiar "crazy quilt" from Ben Joe's second Sandhill home, Shelley's house (211). As the conductor confirms as their train leaves for New York, marriage with Shelley means the one thing for which Ben Joe yearns: "Won't have to change" (266).

If this strategy for dealing, or not dealing, with change and time seems naive, counterproductive, even unhealthy, it is evidently what Ben Joe needs, given his temperament and the expectations forced upon him by society and his family. It is particularly understandable

IF MORNING EVER COMES AND *THE TIN CAN TREE*

in light of the tenuousness of the fictional worlds in this novel and *The Tin Can Tree*. Images of reversal and backward movement abound, as do references to knots, labyrinths, curlicues, and twists. As noted, Ben Joe reads texts placed upside-down, while the Potter sisters reside in a series of mazes; Maisie Hammond and Simon Pike walk backwards; old Mr. Dower lives in constant terror that "someday my intestines will get tied in a bow by accident, like shoelaces" (40); the three-family home is one-half mile from Larksville "as a bird flies," but a full mile by the curving road (8, 6); Ansel Green's pajama legs entangle and trip his brother James. Of course, these are for the most part emblems of personal confusion and feelings of entrapment and helplessness, but more importantly they are manifestations of an entire world seemingly out of control. It is a world so oblivious to the "normal" movement of time and the "normal" kinds of change that a six-year-old girl dies in a tractor accident while the doddering Misses Potter seemingly go on forever.

In both novels Tyler's characters seek desperately to come to grips with this apparently chaotic world, a world not just of change and of passing time—entities which carry at least the suggestion of inevitability and orderliness, respectively—but of seeming fragmentation and inversion. Most of the characters cannot even articulate the problem. Ben Joe, for example, gropingly speaks of his family as square dancers whose pattern is broken when he just misses contact with their hands, while to Shelley he laments that time itself seems fragmented: "the days seem to come in pieces now. They used to be in blocks—all one solid color to them. Sometimes whole *weeks* would be in blocks" (143). Significantly, he visualizes marriage to Shelley as something whole and solid: "Behind his own eyelids the future rolled out like a long, deep rug, as real as the past or the present ever was" (265).

But whether or not they can fathom or articulate the problem, the characters in both novels respond to it instinctively: they constantly seek to detect, and sometimes even to create, an order running counter to the chaos.

For one thing, Tyler's characters rely heavily on rituals, games, and superstitions. Mrs. Pike's aforementioned desire to stop all the clocks in the house, although it may sound desperate, pathetic, or even psychotic, is in fact a traditional sign of mourning, as once was the act of alerting the fruit trees "so that they wouldn't shrivel up" (154, *156*) when someone in the household had died. (One also was expected to notify the honeybees in the family's hive. See John Greenleaf Whittier's 1858 poem, "Telling the Bees.") The rituals of mourning are as meaningful, but as seemingly irrational, as the various acts of superstition in these two novels. Young Jenny Hawkes, for example, had insisted that the bagpiper continue to play his single irritating note in the hope that somehow it would bring back from the dead her father, who had hired him to play his pipe as a joke on his sleeping family. Less poignantly, after re-establishing his relationship with Shelley, Ben Joe "swung three times around the tree on his corner, the way he had always done for good luck when he was small" (156), and he attributes to "black magic" the fact that Shelley's beau began to date his sister Joanne once their own relationship had resumed (204). Even Ben Joe's level-headed Columbia roommate ritualistically buys a new red toothbrush every winter. These people seem to feel that there is underlying this chaotic world a set of well-defined rules. Though these rules may be accessible and meaningful only to particular individuals, they nonetheless betoken an inherent order—and, hence, they hold open the possibility of at least a modicum of personal control over events affecting them.

More telling, however, is the characters' impulse not simply to detect but to *create* meaningful patterns and designs suggestive of orderliness and continuity. This impulse is perhaps most evident in relatively simple objects and images. For example, the various crazy quilts in *If Morning Ever Comes* literally are wholes imaginatively constructed out of pieces. Along the same lines, dressmaker Mrs. Pike consciously arranges cookies in designs on the "little clear sparkly plate" (160, *161*) she reserves for her customers, while the very act of sewing together dresses cut from patterns betokens her urge to create beautiful wholes out of unpromising fragments. Even Ansel's "icebox pizza" (17, *15*), loaded with leftovers, peanut butter, even fruit, is an offbeat manifestation of the impulse to transform otherwise unappetizing and incompatible pieces into usable, appealing entities.

But by far the most significant manifestation of this impulse is the pursuit of the fine arts, and in particular photography. Tyler is insistent that the photograph is a way of stopping change, or freezing time. As "very *remaining* things" (24, 23), photographs seem capable even of staving off that ultimate symbol of change and time, death itself. The Hammond family, for example, insists on James's taking their photograph at each annual reunion, "certain that they and their children were being saved intact for future generations" (56, 55). This conviction leads Connie Hammond to insist that James photograph old Great-Aunt Hattie because she is "fading" fast (65); since she may not live to see next year's reunion, it is urgent that she be "securely boxed" in James's camera (74). But Great-Aunt Hattie's disgust over being forced to pose alone points to the inadequacies of the photograph as a hedge against change, time, and the uncertainties of a chaotic world. As Hattie observes, a photograph is "something flat and of one tone," whereas "everything else is a mingling of things" (71). In fine, a photograph fails to capture or convey the reality of the individual being photographed. Further, the art of photography involves artificiality, distortion, even falsehood. The picture of himself that Ansel Green prefers is a "heroic" pose rather than his usual simpering self reclining on his couch (25, 24). In addition, people become tense and inanimate when being photographed: "I don't hardly recognize you all" (267, 270) says James to the friends and family members who were so lively just before he brought out his camera. And photographs are routinely retouched: little Janice Hammond wants James to make her look *"pretty"* in the reunion photos—"You see what you can do about it" (74, 73), and chances are that he will.[10]

Other art forms do not fare much better. Miss Faye's silhouettes, for example, fail to render meaningful detail, and even they may be "retouched": she adds a point to the top of Joan Pike's silhouetted head, one "that wasn't really there" (266, 270). More dramatically, the statue to Civil War hero Major John Caraway in *The Tin Can Tree* would seem to be a particularly time- and change-resistant recorder of reality; but unfortunately few remember which was "the Big War" and, at just three feet in height, the statue does not convey even the Major's physical appearance, let alone his character or personality (241, 244).

Significantly, the most promising works of art in either novel were made by children. Little Danny Hammond's ceramic saltshaker in the shape of Great-Aunt Hattie's head is three-dimensional (and hence more realistic than a flat photograph); it is accurately rendered (he thoughtfully includes all her wrinkles); and it is useful (the salt comes out of her nostrils). Even James Green, himself a professional photographer, has to admit that this functional art has a distinct edge over photos, which people rarely look at. Even more original and permanent is Janie Rose Pike's tin can tree, which has long outlived her. As with the lollipop-shaped fruit trees which she drew obsessively before creating it (her mother had chided her that "Other children draw houses" [43, 42], it is a unique entity which manages to merge seeming antitheses—things natural and man-made, vegetable and mineral, living and inert—into a meaningful whole. Created, significantly, during Janie Rose's "religious period" and "dedicated ... to God," the tin can tree *has* managed to exert a measure of control over change, time, and death: as Ansel points out, Mr. Pike was mistaken when he "thought he had placed every last bit of her in a hole in the ground" (132, 133). She lives still, and through art of a particular sort: although technically a cross between a piece of sculpture and a mobile, the tin can tree is actually quite similar in nature to a collage. Janie Rose thus has anticipated the activity of the mature Anne Tyler's most notable creator, collage artist Jeremy Pauling of *Celestial Navigation*. Janie Rose's instinctive preference for the collage underscores what Tyler herself was gropingly trying to convey: that like the dots constituting James's photograph of Janie Rose in the Model A Ford, the world *is* fragmented and apparently unfocused—but not thereby meaningless. With a broad enough perspective and sufficient imagination, one can indeed perceive it as purposeful and whole.

IF MORNING EVER COMES AND *THE TIN CAN TREE*

Broadly speaking, both *If Morning Ever Comes* and *The Tin Can Tree* have much to commend them. The contemporary reviewers' generally favorable responses were rooted not only in the appreciative surprise that they were written by a woman, and a young one at that, but also in the fact that they are evidence of an imaginative intelligence responding to difficult questions facing all mankind. This is not to say, of course, that the two books are perfect. Technically, they are often shaky. Tyler resorts too readily to the "he-looked-in-the-mirror-and-saw ..." technique for describing Ben Joe Hawkes (11). She relies too much on clothing as a projection of personality: between the flaming red dress, gold hoop earrings, and far-flung raven hair, we know all that we need to know of Joanne Hawkes' checkered reputation. And she uses too often those Proustian triggers of memory: standing by the railing, Ben Joe suddenly recalls that it was at this same spot that he heard the bagpiper and learned of his father's death. (Read: "Insert flashback here.") Rather more seriously, the themes underlying the two books seem not always to have been fully thought out. There is, for example, a palpable confusion and tenuousness underlying the exploration of the efficacy of art in *The Tin Can Tree*, as there is regarding the idea of Ben Joe's "reversibility" in *If Morning Ever Comes*. (The reader is inclined to agree with Shelley that he talks as if he were a raincoat [149–50].) Nor is Tyler's strong suit the endings of her novels. Is Ben Joe's elopement with Shelley Domer an affirmative step? A childish impulse? Both? Neither? And how should the reader respond when the group photo at the end of *The Tin Can Tree*—one that pointedly excludes Joan Pike[11]—is said to confirm that "They were going to stay this way, [Joan] and all the rest of them, not because of anyone else but because it was what they had chosen, what they would keep a strong tight hold of" (269–70, 273)? Were they really making their own choices? And will those choices prove to be for the best? One suspects that Tyler knows, and one can only lament that she does not provide the kinds of information and guideposts that her readers need to respond properly to her fictional vision. In nine more novels created over a generation of writing, Anne Tyler will resurrect these technical matters, themes, and ideas, will work through and refine them in ways that are uniquely her own.

Notes

1. Wendy Lamb, "An Interview with Anne Tyler," *Iowa Journal of Literary Studies* 3 (1981): 64.

2. Lamb 64.

3. [Unsigned Review], *Time* 85 (1 January 1965): 71.

4. Haskel Frankel, "Closing a Family Wound," *Saturday Review* 48 (20 November 1965): 50. Frankel makes a suggestive comparison between *The Tin Can Tree* and James Agee's *A Death in the Family* [1957]: "the Agee novel does offer a clue to why one only respects *The*

IF MORNING EVER COMES AND *THE TIN CAN TREE*

Tin Can Tree without being deeply moved by it. Mr. Agee gave us time to meet the father before death was allowed to remove him so that we could grieve for him with his family. Miss Tyler introduces us to the Pikes after Janie Rose's passing. We have never known her alive so cannot mourn her dead. We can observe and sympathize but we are still outsiders during the period of adjustment. As a result, what lingers longest in the mind when the last page of *The Tin Can Tree* has been turned is the savor of the author's talent rather than a novel's content" (50). Frankel's point would be well taken if Tyler's primary interest had been Janie Rose herself. However, it seems clear that her true concern is the fact of death itself, rather than the character of the victim, and the impact of that fact on the survivors.

5. As Orville Prescott observes in regard to the Hawkes "womenfolk," "There are too many of them for all to be characterized in depth, but their collective personality is striking" ("Return to the Hawkes Family," *The New York Times*, 114 [11 November 1964]: 41). Tyler's interest in the "collective personality" of a family may explain her frequent use of twins. The Hawkes household includes twins Lisa and Jane.

6. Anne G. Jones, for example, has written that "Ben Joe's disturbing desire for his sister [presumably Joanne] expresses the family reluctance to seek satisfaction outside its borders" ("Home at Last, and Homesick Again: The Ten Novels of Anne Tyler," *The Hollins Critic* 23 [April 1986]: 3). It would be difficult to build a case that Ben Joe feels incestuous urges towards any of his sisters. However, drab, barely individualized Shelley Domer does seem similar to the Hawkes girls, so she must have been comfortingly familiar to Ben Joe. Further, the fact that her beau John Horner had dated Joanne Hawkes and resumed the relationship when Ben Joe began to date Shelley again would suggest that there is a double romantic triangle at work in the novel (Joanne-John-Shelley/John-Shelley-Ben Joe) which could conceivably be seen as indirectly incestuous.

7. Jonathan Yardley, "Anne Tyler's Family Circles," *Washington Post Book World* (25 August 1985): 3.

UNDERSTANDING ANNE TYLER

8. The significance of the novel's title is explained, rather too blatantly, in Chapter 14. Dr. Hawkes's story of the "silly-minded boy" (225) named Quality Jones does illustrate the limits of interpersonal communication, the capacity of familial love to disrupt as much as to comfort, and the universality of the fear of darkness and its attendant uncertainties. What seems more striking about the novel's title is the implication of insomnia, a malady from which Tyler herself has suffered, and which is in keeping with the recurring novelistic pattern of inversion. The Hawkes family seems most active at night, when they should be sleeping.

9. John Allan Long, "'New' Southern Novel," *Christian Science Monitor* 57 (21 January 1965): 9.

10. It is difficult to agree with Anne R. Zahlan that in the character of James Green, Tyler "introduces the dilemma of the artist whose creativity demands a self-centered solitude his humanity rejects" ("Anne Tyler," in Joseph M. Flora and Robert Bain, eds., *Fifty Southern Writers After 1900: A Bio-Bibliographical Sourcebook* [Westport, Connecticut: Greenwood Press, 1987]: 493). Green seems less insistently an "artist" than, say, Jeremy Pauling of *Celestial Navigation;* most of his pictures are taken in a workmanlike fashion for the Larksville newspaper. Further, his intensive care for his brother and his obvious affection for both Joan and Simon hardly betoken "self-centered solitude."

11. Doris Betts argues that by photographing "the family," Joan Pike "makes visual her absence from it" ("The Fiction of Anne Tyler," *Southern Quarterly* 21 [Summer 1983]: 33). This would be convincing only if the photograph did not include Miss Lucy and Miss Faye Potter, Ansel Green, or James Green—none of whom is part of "the family." It would seem more accurate to argue that by setting up a physical barrier (a camera lens) between herself and the others, Joan is confirming that she, having neither siblings, parents, nor husband in the microcosm of the three-family house, is effectively an outsider and will always remain so. That she evidently chooses to remain there despite this status is a situation to which the reader is uncertain how to respond.

CHAPTER THREE

A Slipping-Down Life

Soon after the birth of her second daughter in 1967, Anne Tyler began work on a third novel. The new story proved to be disappointing, however, and so *Winter Birds, Winter Apples* remains unpublished.[1] Tyler was much happier with what was to become her third published novel, *A Slipping-Down Life* (1970). Reportedly she still speaks of it "with great tenderness"; and although she acknowledges that this novel is "flawed," she nonetheless feels that it "represents, for me, a certain brave stepping forth."[2] In part, that stepping forth involves technical improvement. As Doris Betts has observed, in *A Slipping-Down Life* Tyler made a radical departure from the first two novels by expanding her "surface time span" to encompass a full year instead of just a few days. Further, there is a reduction in the number of characters depicted, as if Tyler were "abandoning the experiment with mere numbers in favor of experimenting with intense individual portraits." These portraits "outline" Tyler's characters with "darker lines" than ever before—an ideal metaphor for a novelist with an affinity for the fine arts, and an apt way of conveying the vividness and substantiality of this novel's characters.[3] Even such minor characters as Clotelia, Mrs. Harrison, and Paul Ogle, the photographer for the local newspaper, are sharply etched and far more memorable than, say, the sisters of Ben Joe Hawkes. But beyond these technical improvements, *A Slipping-Down Life* also evinces Tyler's brave stepping forth in the selection and presentation of themes. Although still clearly evident are the first two novels' interest in the dynamics of the individual and the family, man's incapacity to communicate, his responses to change and passing time, and his search for meaningful patterns in life, Tyler seems more willing in this third novel to examine their complexity, their sources, and their interconnectedness. In particular, she takes an uncompromising look at the socializing function of popular culture, the nature of marriage as an institution, and the capacity of popular culture and marriage either to nurture or to thwart the development of a healthy sense of self. To her credit, Tyler is able to probe these complex and problematical issues using a relatively straightforward narration, and to conclude her novel with an ending that is affirmative without being either facile or sentimental.

Far more than with either *If Morning Ever Comes* or *The Tin Can Tree*, the world of *A Slipping-Down Life* is one of popular culture. References to rock concerts, radio, television, magazines, and motion pictures abound. But although these serve to anchor the novel

A SLIPPING-DOWN LIFE

in the America of the 1960s, they are more important as keys to understanding what the characters do—and why. For the various media of popular culture would appear to have usurped the vital role of socializer from such traditional sources as the family, school, and the Church. Most of the processes of socialization, and in particular the instilling of community-wide values and standards of conduct, have been assumed by the media. This phenomenon is most apparent in the realm of love and romance.

To be thin is to be worthy of love. Such is the message, overt or subliminal, that Evie Decker has been sent all her life. Significantly, she personally does not seem to mind being obese, and in fact she evidently feels that it is both normal and natural for her to be overweight. But unfortunately hers is a media-based world which is notoriously intolerant of the somatotype that is so integral to Evie's identity. Unable to buy anything but unstylish "fat clothes," Evie plods through the novel in 40-D bras, sensible oxford shoes, a frumpy coat, and muu-muus. She can only listen as other, thinner girls pursue dates with rock stars in contests sponsored by pulpy teen magazines, and can only watch stolidly as attractive Fay-Jean Lindsay, inspired by *Silver Screen* magazine, vamps her way into the arms, backseats, and beds of assorted swains in Pulqua and Farinia, North Carolina. Even Evie's father, a sporadically perceptive man, recognizes that physical attractiveness is a condition of affection in this world: "There are *plenty* of nice boys in the world. Just give yourself time. You're a sweet-looking girl, after all, and when you lose a, when you're older, boys are going to fall all over themselves for you, take my word" (47, *43–44*). Likewise, Drum's marriage proposal, such as it is, is preambled by a recommendation that Evie use the "slenderizing place" in nearby Tar City (134, *129*).

If popular culture dictates who is to be loved, it also dictates the nature of that love. The Deckers' black housemaid Clotelia carefully studies the soap operas on television, even going so far as to talk to the characters, whose own lives seem to be ceaseless rounds of passion. Mr. Decker, well aware of society's distortion of romance, supplies Evie with magazines that "had nothing to do with rock music, or teen-agers, or even love" (58, *55*). But even more than magazines, the most potent purveyor of distortive attitudes about romance, particularly for teen-agers, is rock music.

Evie first becomes attracted to Drumstrings Casey when she hears him interviewed on the radio. The program is called "Sweetheart Time," and indeed it is time for Evie, at seventeen, to be interested in a man, whether or not the world around her feels she is attractive enough to deserve him. "Sweetheart Time" is hosted by an older disc jockey named Herbert who, like Evie's father, seems literally on another wavelength: he does not understand the teen ritual of "dedicating" records, and can barely carry on a conversation with Drum, the reluctant interviewee. Able only to hear him,

A SLIPPING-DOWN LIFE

Evie seems drawn instinctively to yet another young person who cannot communicate with a father figure, while being unable to visualize him enables her to respond more completely to the persona Drum has so carefully cultivated: the ultra-cool rock star. He seems mysteriously creative, laconic, superior—in short, the personification of sexuality as it is understood by that aspect of popular culture geared to teen-agers. Evie is smitten. She tracks him down at a rock show in the Stardust Movie Theatre, and then to the Unicorn roadhouse, where one fateful night she carves his name into her forehead with fingernail scissors.

It is a rare instance of violence for a Tyler novel, but its extremity and sensationalism should not overshadow the fact that it is, for its era, understandable as an expression of affection. The popular culture of the 1960s frequently linked violence with romance, particularly in such successful musical recordings as "Tell Laura I Love Her," "Teen Angel," "Patches," and "Ode to Billy Joe." Young love seemed to lead unswervingly to car wrecks and drownings, according to popular music of the early- and mid-1960s,[4] while the acid rock and hard rock of the late 1960s—a movement of which Drum Casey seems to be in the vanguard—retained the linking of passion and violence while omitting the earlier music's cloying sentimentality. Evie's self-mutilation, based on an actual incident in which a Texas teen slashed her forehead with "Elvis,"[5] is thus much in keeping with the bizarre norm conveyed by teen-targeted media. And yet it seems an unnatural act, so much so that the emergency room physician questions Evie's sanity. To an earlier society, it would have seemed the act of one possessed; and that would appear to be Tyler's intent in presenting Drumstrings Casey as a figure as old as literature itself, the "demon lover."

Certainly he looks the part. Repeatedly termed "dark," Drum dresses all in black denim. Instead of walking, like a snake he is said to "glide" or "slide" (e.g., 16, 14). He wears reflective sunglasses "made of a silvery black that mirrored Evie perfectly and turned his own face, what you could see of it, into something as hard and as opaque as the glasses themselves" (51, 48). Drum's unorthodox singing style, called "talking out" or "speaking out," seems to be conveying a secret message: "Is he saying something? Is there something underneath it? Is he speaking in code?" (35, 33). Also like a true devil, Drum seems enveloped in an unnatural circle of chilly air. And he mysteriously leaves no physical imprint on the cushions of the porch swing on which he sleeps. He seems sexy, alluring, powerful; and Clotelia articulates what Evie cannot: that she had hoped her demon lover "'would come riding up and spirit her away'" that summer (63, 60). His failure to do so suggests that Tyler has chosen to develop the motif of the rock-star-cum-demon-lover only up to a certain point. Beyond that point, she exposes it for what it is: a farcically inappropriate, but nonetheless potentially destructive, charade.

A SLIPPING-DOWN LIFE

For on the most basic level Drumstrings Casey, contrary to the customary practice of the demon lover, does not pursue this fat virgin. He is interested in Evie only until he establishes that she is not a "newspaper lady" (52, *48*)—unlike devils, would-be rock stars need publicity—and he takes no responsibility for, or pleasure in, her mutilation. Indeed, he is actually annoyed—not that she did it, but that she carved his last name instead of "Drum": after all, "There're thousands of Caseys around" (54, *51*). In addition, instead of Pandemonium, he lives in a faded Victorian house with his parents, and he drives the battered family Dodge. With his "bony, scraped" wrists, nicotine-stained fingers (129, *123*), and richly warranted bouts of professional insecurity, Drumstrings Casey quickly emerges as what he is: a slick-looking kid with a shallow gimmick and little talent.

Evie is aware of most of this when she elopes with him, just as he is well aware that she has nothing in common with the 1960s' adolescent understanding of what constitutes a desirable girlfriend or wife. This apparent two-fold rejection of the powerful media-based idea of romance points, at least on Evie's part, to a spark of originality and individuality, one that will enable her to emerge from her failed marriage unscathed, even empowered by the experience. But before she can reach this state, Evie must endure the painful rite of passage of a marriage that was doomed before it began.

Why people marry whom they do is an issue of

continuing fascination to Anne Tyler. Anne G. Jones has argued that Tyler is particularly intrigued by "the apparently accidental, almost quirky ways in which marriages (hence families) are made,"[6] but in fact the forces underlying the marriage of Drum and Evie are less "accidental" or "quirky" than they are complex. Barbara A. Bannon in *Publishers Weekly* attributes the match to mutual "propinquity and loneliness," and to be sure Drum does seem as alienated and frustrated as Evie—qualities which, argues Mary Ellen Brooks, are evident in the lack of coherence in his "talking out," a form of non-communication that becomes increasingly incomprehensible as the novel progresses.[7] At the same time, marriage to Drum fulfills emotional needs in Evie while resolving certain practical difficulties. On the most basic level, she dreads returning to high school in the fall. Marriage gives her the perfect excuse for increasingly frequent absences, while on the days she does attend class, she is a kind of celebrity: "people stared at her and were too polite. She didn't mind. She had known that getting married would set her apart" (154, *149*). Further, Drum lets Evie talk as much as she wishes, something that was not indulged in the Decker household, while having a husband means she no longer need fear growing old as a spinster.

Drum's motives for marrying Evie are even more complex and insubstantial than these. Practically speaking, he needs some place to live, replete with "coziness" (155, *150*) and breakfast biscuits, since the Caseys had

A SLIPPING-DOWN LIFE

disowned him after a ruckus at the Parisian. He also needs the kind of emotional support that Evie continues to be willing to provide. She apologizes for having said, in a moment of anger, that he had no talent, and in fact declares "I could listen all day when you play." " 'Well, then,' said Drum. It seemed to be what he had come for" (123, *118*). Drum also feels that Evie would bring him good luck at a moment when his career is foundering, while at the same time showing the mother who rejected him that "I'm settled and done with her" (151, *146*). Marriage also would bring him something for which most Tyler characters yearn: change. "I feel like things are just petering out all around me and I want to get married to someone I like and have me a house and *change*. Make a change. Isn't that enough [reason to marry]?" (135, *130*). Apparently so; and especially during a heatwave, when people are not known for making intelligent decisions.

Not one of these multiple motives for Drum and Evie's marriage is detected by outsiders. Mr. Decker assumes Drum married his daughter as compensation for her mutilation, while Mrs. Casey assumes it is her son's way of showing his appreciation for Evie's support of his career. Of even greater interest, the usual motive attributed to teen elopements, sexual passion, is not at issue. Drum's facade of rock-star sexuality notwithstanding, their courtship is passionless. Though Evie had yearned for a normal courtship with "double dates and dances and matching shirts," all she gets is a

kiss from Drum's "cool blank lips" to seal their engagement (136, *131*). Once they are married, coitus proves
bumbling and tepid:

She had overheard more in the girls' gym than she had
yet found out with Drum in the papery bedroom. Their
love-making was sudden and awkward, complicated by
pitch dark and a twisted nightgown and the welter of
sheets and blankets that Evie kept covering herself
with. (154, *149*)

By the time Evie discovers him in bed with the tireless
Fay-Jean, his demonic black outfit removed to reveal
"yellowed underpants and an undershirt with a hole in
the chest, its neckband frayed" (215, *208*), it is clear that
the marriage is over.

But this state of affairs is not as tragic as one might
expect—or, more precisely, it is not equally tragic for
both young people. For in depicting Drum and Evie's
abortive marriage, Tyler relies upon a fictional motif familiar to readers of Henry James's *The Sacred Fount* or
F. Scott Fitzgerald's *Tender Is the Night:* the transference
of husband/wife vitality. Drum's marriage to Evie, far
from solving all his problems, seems only to exacerbate
them. If he were only sporadically employed before the
elopement, he is essentially unemployed once the marriage gets under way. Further, although marriage had
initially brought out his non-demonic streak of domesticity, one characterized by an overwhelming urge to

A SLIPPING-DOWN LIFE

install can openers and toothbrush holders, Drum rapidly settles into slovenliness. Even more cogently, the bouts of depression and professional insecurity which he had suffered occasionally quickly crystallize, after marriage, into chronic despair:

"What is the point in me sitting here strumming? I'll never get anywhere. I ain't but nineteen years old and already leading a slipping-down life . . . Feels like I have hit my peak and passed it. I was just a fool to ever hope to be famous." (176–77, *170*)

Not yet twenty years old, Drumstrings Casey is less a has-been than a never-was.

His wife Evie, in contrast, seems to thrive in marriage. If she had been lost in the world of the high schooler, she is at home in the domestic world of adulthood. Unlike Drum, whose domesticity proves as superficial as his rock star persona, Evie rises to the occasion of caring for her husband (such as he is) and their home (though it is only a tar paper shack). With marriage, the teen-targeted popular culture which she had been unable or unwilling to accept is replaced by a housewife-targeted one, and Evie eagerly embraces its values and standards of conduct as voiced by the *Ladies' Home Journal* and *Good Housekeeping*. To be sure, much of the knowledge she thus acquires is of questionable value, such as the importance of coating ash trays with a thin film of floor wax before one's company arrives.

But she also learns about adult interaction, something to which she had not been exposed in the single-parent Decker household. This new brand of popular culture offers her guidance, for example, on how to react when Drum opposes having a working wife ("She had read in *Family Circle* about how wives needed tact at times like this" [169, *163*]), and it gives her the recipes—and the confidence—necessary to engineer a conciliatory dinner with two sets of in-laws understandably upset by their children's elopement.

Evie's rousing success as a wife and hostess does not, however, leave her blinded by the dictates of the media: much as she had consciously rejected many aspects of the teen-targeted popular culture, she now selectively rejects those aspects of housewife-targeted popular culture that would render her helpless and dependent on her husband. She does not, for example, suffer emotional collapse when she discovers Drum's adultery. Neither blinded by love nor brainwashed by the 1960s' exhortation to "Stand By Your Man," Evie simply realizes that it would be easier to raise a child with a husband and father in the household. Only when Drum refuses to fulfill those roles, only when he opts to remain in the shack wallowing in self-pity, does Evie walk out on him. For it is now clear that Drum, "whose personality hovers at that point of fusion where cool-and dull-wittedness are one,"[8] is not able to range beyond the egocentricity of a child—and Evie already has her hands full with the real child soon to be born.

A SLIPPING-DOWN LIFE

In the final analysis it is arguably the pregnancy, far more than the marriage itself, that brings out the best in Evie. In an incisive study published in the *New England Review and Bread Loaf Quarterly*, Margaret Morganroth Gullette observes that "for most of Tyler's women, the baby, not the husband, is the true sign of entry into responsible adulthood." Thus the importance of the accumulation of physical objects and furniture, like tip-proof high-chairs, those emblems of the acceptance of the restrictions and responsibilities of the mature individual. Though not speaking directly of *A Slipping-Down Life*, Gullette observes further that in some Tyler novels, motherhood proves to be "a happy *instinct*, a gift of the life course,"[9] and that certainly appears to be the case with Evie. Motherhood seems to have been the goal for which she had subconsciously striven from the opening of the novel. She seemed to know just from hearing him on the radio that Drum Casey was to be her mate, and she did on impulse—or was it on instinct?—the one thing guaranteed to get his attention: she carved his name in her forehead. This self-mutilation is, as suggested earlier, a manifestation of the media-cued yoking of teen romance and violence; but it is also, in a distorted way, a kind of marriage. For Evie has done melodramatically what, until recently, all women did automatically upon marriage: they take their mates' names as their own. Or, more precisely, they take their *last* names, rejecting the identity of "daughter" in favor of "wife" in rejecting the father's family name in a kind of symbolic suicide of the daughterly self.[10] Though Drum would have preferred Evie to carve "Drum" (her forehead wasn't broad enough for "Drumstrings"), Evie seems to have realized instinctively that what she needed to take as her own was the surname Casey—that is, the socially accepted proof of the woman's marriage and the legitimacy of any children she may have. "[Casey] *is* my name" (219, *212*) she retorts as she walks out on her husband, but that identity has less to do with one Bertram "Drumstrings" Casey than with the symbolic roles of wife and mother that come with marriage. In marrying him, both symbolically through the mutilation and legally through the elopement, Evie has announced publicly her decision to accept those roles; and if his childishness and lethargy compel her to abandon the role of wife, she still can immerse herself in the role of mother.

Indeed, without pressing the matter too much, Tyler suggests that the ineffectual Drum had minimal input into the Big Event. The decision to have a child was entirely Evie's: "flying in the face of all logical objections," she yearns for motherhood, visualizing it as "a shaft of yellow light through her mind, like a door opening" (177, *170*). Drum knows nothing of this, falling asleep oblivious to his wife's urges. Significantly, Evie already *looks* pregnant—as indeed she has looked for her entire life of obesity. Even before she articulates her dream ("She wanted to get pregnant" [177, *170*]), she instinctively takes a job in the library, an appropriately quiet, sedentary occupation[11] which requires that she wear "a blue smock" (169, *162*)—an outfit curiously reminiscent of maternity clothes. And not long after she secures the ideal job for a mother-to-be, she is, almost as if by her own force of will, decidedly pregnant. When she finally gets around to mentioning the baby to Drum, it is not a happy announcement but a statement of fact which, Evie feels, should be a major impetus in their move to her childhood home, left to her upon the sudden death of her father. When the fact of impending parenthood does not convince Drum to leave the tar paper shack, Evie walks out on him.

Evie Decker Casey, protofeminist, has taken what she needed from a husband—a socially acceptable married name, some sperm—and marched back to the Decker house to raise her baby alone. What she is doing requires courage and a strong sense of self, qualities which were not evident in the Evie at the opening of the novel. Indeed, she seems to have undergone a complete inversion by the story's end. But that impression is not quite accurate. Those admirable qualities had always been within her; but like her oval fingernails and narrow nose, they somehow had been overlooked in a world which posits overweight teens as lacking in character and willpower. But the same heaviness that is so undesirable in an adolescent is just fine for a pregnant matron, whom society treats with remarkable respect and deference. Social norms derived from popular culture have shifted far more than Evie herself, and the

UNDERSTANDING ANNE TYLER

only real inversion to occur on her part is her perception of herself and the world. In carving Drum's name in reverse, Evie does seem to confirm that, at that stage, she was looking at matters 180° off: as Mary Ellen Brooks argues, "it is as though she sees people and situations backwards, like the letters on her forehead."[12] But by the end of the novel she sees Fay-Jean, Drum, and the rest of her world rightly, and it enables her to slam the door on her friend and to leave her husband without a moment's hesitation. More importantly, Evie sees *herself* rightly—and that would lend credence to the argument of several critics that the baby she is carrying is the true Evie: in effect, she "gives birth to herself."[13] Almost as if to confirm this, she goes so far as to say that "*I* didn't cut my forehead. Someone else did" (220, 212). That "someone else" is not, as she maintains, another teen, but rather her earlier self, now dead.

The ending of *A Slipping-Down Life* is thus an affirmative one. Essentially a parable of the evolution of one woman's strong, healthy sense of identity, the novel does not end on an "inconclusive" note, nor is it quite accurate to say that it "underscores the passivity and shallowness of Evie's and Casey's lives."[14] For though Drum admittedly is more passive and shallow than ever at the end of the novel, Evie has moved beyond juvenile angst and "slipped down into [a] life" of adult responsibility.[15] If it is not a flawless vision—and even Tyler herself "has subsequently confessed to a de-

A SLIPPING-DOWN LIFE

sire to know how 'Evie Decker's baby turned out' "[16]—it is nonetheless meant to be a positive one. From this point on, strong women able to raise their families alone and to deal with the crises and impediments of daily life will be a salient feature of Anne Tyler's novels. This character type, which ultimately will include such women as Pearl Tull of *Dinner at the Homesick Restaurant* and Muriel Pritchett of *The Accidental Tourist*, is explored in its formative stage in the person of Elizabeth Abbott, the resident handyperson of Tyler's next novel, *The Clock Winder*.

Notes

1. Anne R. Zahlan, "Anne Tyler," in Joseph M. Flora and Robert Bain, eds., *Fifty Southern Writers After 1900: A Bio-Bibliographical Sourcebook* (Westport, Connecticut: Greenwood Press, 1987): 492.

2. Paul Binding, "Anne Tyler," in *Separate Country: A Literary Journey through the American South* (New York & London: Paddington Press, 1979): 203. Tyler is quoted in Mary Ellen Brooks, "Anne Tyler," in *The Dictionary of Literary Biography*, Vol. 6: *American Novelists Since World War II* (Detroit: Gale Research, 1980): 340.

3. Doris Betts, "The Fiction of Anne Tyler," *Southern Quarterly* 21 (Summer 1983): 28.

4. Despite the references to David's psychedelic jeep (78, 74), hard rock (7, 4), and Black Panther rallies (209, 202), all of which would place the novel in the mid- to late-1960s, Tyler seems deliberately to suggest that the small North Carolina towns of its setting exist almost in an early-1960s time warp. Fay-Jean, for example, wears "a

skirt and blouse decorated with poodles on loops of real chain" (24, 22), an outfit popular around 1960. This apparent anachronism would suggest that there is a spectrum of pop music from which the young people may choose, ranging from the sentimental love ballads of the earliest part of the decade to the acid rock of its end. In being attracted to Drumstrings Casey, then, Evie is showing herself to be an original, well ahead of her time.

5. Marguerite Michaels, "Anne Tyler, Writer 8:05 to 3:30," *New York Times Book Review* (8 May 1977): 43. Tyler seems deliberately to underscore the implied connection between Drum and Elvis Presley by describing how "Drum slid his pelvis easily beneath the spangled guitar" (179, 173). Paul Binding makes the valid observation that in "our current age," rock music "is a principal medium by which a male asserts his attractions and powers over the female (a medium which moreover originated in the South)" (204). Presley's Southern background would, then, do much to explain the appeal of someone like Drum Casey, who in his own way is emulating the Mississippi-born King of Rock and Roll.

6. Anne G. Jones, "Home at Last, and Homesick Again: The Ten Novels of Anne Tyler," *The Hollins Critic* 23 (April 1986): 3.

7. Barbara A. Bannon, [rev. of *A Slipping-Down Life*], *Publishers Weekly*, 197 (12 January 1970): 59; Brooks 340.

8. Arthur Edelstein, "Art and Artificiality in Some Recent Fiction," *Southern Review* NS 9 (July 1973): 742.

9. Margaret Morganroth Gullette, "The Tears (and Joys) Are in the Things: Adulthood in Anne Tyler's Novels," *New England Review and Bread Loaf Quarterly* 7 (Spring 1985): 327–28, emphasis added.

10. The notion of symbolic suicide would explain the recurring references to Evie's wrists. In the hospital after the mutilation, Evie holds up both wrists in front of the mirror "and turned the blue-veined, glistening insides of them toward the glass. Then she backed away, very slowly. But when she was as far as she could get, pressed against the wall behind her, the letters [on her forehead] still stood out ragged and black. 'Casey.' A voice inside her read the name out,

A SLIPPING-DOWN LIFE

coolly: 'Casey'" (48–49, 45). The doctor who reluctantly signs her discharge papers is startled to find Evie "alone in the middle of her room, surveying the insides of her wrists" (55, 52) as if she expected to see the slash marks there instead of on her face. Her father's colleagues at the high school hear incorrectly that Evie had "slashed her wrists with a movie star's initials" (57, 53–54). And Drum longs to tell people that Evie had in fact committed suicide, "Finished what she started" (133, 128).

11. Interestingly, Anne Tyler herself recalls the pleasure of working in a library as a Russian bibliographer, where her days were spent sitting on a stool sorting out catalogue cards. See "Still Just Writing," in Janet Sternburg, ed., *The Writer on Her Work* (New York: Norton, 1980): 7.

12. Brooks 340.

13. "[A]t the end of the novel, Evie gives birth to herself, belatedly, by separating herself from Drum: she 'felt something pulled out of her that he had drawn, like a hard deep string.' Evie has fed on Drum from the start, when she eagerly listened as he played on the radio. In this novel the 'string' of that symbiosis is severed, to allow the chance for autonomous growth" (Jones 4). The suggestion that Evie is a sort of incubus who "feeds" on Drum is not quite accurate, though it obviously is related to the concept of the transference of husband/wife vitality. Even before the marriage, Drum was deteriorating while Evie was gaining strength and confidence. Their marriage seems essentially to have accelerated ongoing processes, particularly in the case of Drum.

14. Brooks 340.

15. Edelstein 742. Since it is Drum rather than Evie who declares he is leading a "slipping-down life" (177, 170), it would appear initially that Edelstein is offering an inappropriate interpretation of the title. On the other hand, the process of slipping down need not always be negative. It can mean a movement towards a more stable and settled level, away from the high pitch of adolescent angst suffered by Evie during the first half of the novel. It would appear, then, that Tyler's

novel traces a two-fold slipping-down: the negative one experienced by Drum, and the more positive one enjoyed by Evie.

16. Quoted in Zahlan 494.

CHAPTER FOUR

The Clock Winder

There are times when it seems almost impossible that Anne Tyler has been lauded for her subtlety as a writer. It is she, after all, who places that modern-day Hester Prynne, Evie Decker—the blood-red scarlet letters on her forehead instead of her breast as a sign of her socially unsanctioned desire to love—in a modest house on Hawthorne Street. And it is she who in *The Clock Winder* (1972) gives the family name "Emerson" to that eccentric clan of Baltimoreans whose story rings changes on that central Emersonian credo, the need for self-reliance. In the case of her fourth novel, one wonders whether Tyler mistrusts the perceptiveness of her reader, who cannot help but notice the number of times the word "rely" appears in the text (e.g., "I should have known better than to rely on you. You or *anyone*" [72, 81]); or whether Tyler harbors a more fundamental mistrust of her ability to handle her own material.

Perhaps, in retrospect, both doubts are justifiable. Almost as much as *A Slipping-Down Life*, *The Clock Winder* has inexplicably been classified as a book for juve-

UNDERSTANDING ANNE TYLER

nile readers,[1] a group not generally noted for either a large measure of self-reliance or a firm grounding in Transcendental thought. And there are times when *The Clock Winder* does indeed seem to be spinning out of control, despite such anchoring devices as the central metaphor of the clocks or the sectioning of the decade-long action into six blocks carefully labeled by date. The apparent lack of cohesion is so striking that one tends to agree with Martin Levin that the novel "pursues a serpentine way, and any bend in the road might just as well be marked finis."[2] But all questions of audience and structure aside, there does seem to be underlying *The Clock Winder* considerable ambivalence regarding the precise nature of self-reliance and the possibility of ever attaining it in a world vastly unlike that of the Sage of Concord.

As the story opens, the characters would appear to be on a kind of continuum of self-reliance. The Emerson clan's nominal matriarch, Mrs. Pamela Carter Emerson, is recently widowed and essentially helpless. She prefers to think otherwise. Mrs. Emerson instantaneously fires Richard, the black handyman, for urinating on her roses, vowing to care for her home all by herself; and she just as suddenly decides single-handedly to store away for the season every piece of outdoor furniture to be found on the extensive grounds. But both assertions of self-reliance, although sincerely intended, backfire. As she admits immediately after the firing, the elderly Mrs. Emerson cannot take personal care of her mansion

THE CLOCK WINDER

and its gardens, any more than she can repeatedly drag chairs and tables across her curiously wild backyard to the garage. Self-reliance on its most basic level, the ability to perform simple domestic tasks, is alien to Mrs. Emerson by both upbringing and temperament. Born to the prosperous Carter family, she depends completely upon hired help to take care of such imposing matters as cooking and cutting flowers: typical of her ineffectuality is her attention to a vase of marigolds, "which she spent minutes rearranging, changing nothing" (6, 9). She is even less self-reliant when it comes to the more mechanical impediments of modern life. She has great difficulty driving cars, is frozen in terror when a slice of bread gets caught in her presumably deadly electric toaster, and is totally overwhelmed by the multitude of clocks in the Emerson home. Unable to determine how to wind them in synchronization, she resents the seeming self-reliance of these mechanical objects: "What was the meaning of these endless rooms of clocks, efficiently going about their business while she twisted her hands in front of them?" (5, 8).

Not surprisingly, her grown children do not fare much better, although their lack of self-reliance points more obviously to the problem central to Mrs. Emerson's own woes: the inability to establish a strong emotional and spiritual core from which to deal with people and events around them. Her son Andrew, for example, seems barely functional. He is dependent on a psychiatrist who feels he must protect the young man from

the world's vicissitudes, most particularly those origi-
nating in the Emerson family. Rarely is he permitted to
go home. Likewise, young Peter, having emotionally
been left behind as his siblings moved to their third-
floor rooms upon reaching adolescence, is left a
"gloomy" (259, *287*) man whose Vietnam experiences
only harden his sense of alienation, helplessness, and
intimidation. Daughter Margaret, whose elopement
with the grocery delivery boy Jimmy Joe would seem to
betoken acute self-reliance, had stood by numbly as
Mrs. Emerson literally packed her bags and forced her
to leave her husband just five weeks after the wedding.
Margaret in her second marriage still cries—not so
much for Jimmy Joe as for her incapacity to take a stand
against her mother. Even the seemingly well-adjusted
Timothy, living alone in a Baltimore apartment and attending medical school, is utterly lacking in self-reliance. Essentially imprisoned in an apartment so
"curtained, carpeted, and upholstered" that it had "a
smothered look" (84, *94*), Timothy is training to become
a doctor only because this is what his mother demands:
"faced with blood, his stomach froze and his throat
closed up and he wondered why his mother expected
so much of him" (63, *72*). Constantly brooding on death,
including the alleged death-by-flushing of his pet gerbil,
Timothy decides to engage in the most twistedly self-
reliant act possible: to kill himself. Even that, significantly, is not purely an act of the self, since the gun
seems to have been activated as much by Elizabeth's

THE CLOCK WINDER

"lunge" to stop him (94, *106*) as by his pulling the trigger.

At first glance, Elizabeth Abbott would appear to be a paragon of self-reliance, especially when measured against the Emersons; and most critics tout her for her "unconventional self" and her "independence and sensitivity,"[3] Emersonian qualities indeed. And certainly these appraisals seem borne out by the text. She literally rescues Mrs. Emerson from the challenges of storing patio furniture, and moves into the house to embark on a career of cleaning gutters, glazing windows, replacing knobs, and assembling toys as lures for the non-visiting Emerson grandchildren. And she certainly seems to have a healthy sense of independence and originality, fighting Mrs. Emerson's determination to make her a housekeeper/cook instead of a handyman, and working to earn money to return to school in the fall. Very commendable. But each one of these evidences of self-reliance is a sham. Elizabeth has no intention of returning to college, where her grades are quite poor. Far from being "Miss Fix-It" (55, *64*), Elizabeth is a self-admitted bumbler whose seemingly encyclopedic knowledge of household repairs is due mostly to a careful reading of printed instructions, some practical advice from the local hardware dealer, and the consulting of *The Complete Home Repairman* which she keeps concealed in her bureau drawer (77–78, *87*). Most dramatically, her rescue of Mrs. Emerson, far from suggesting strength of character, betokens weakness. Unwilling to go to her job interview with the O'Donnells, she lets herself be sidetracked into an open-ended commitment to a family about which she knows nothing. It's a weakness that even Mrs. Emerson detects: "no *vivacity*, that was it, and this tendency to drift into whatever offered itself" (18, 22). Without goals, skills, or emotional resiliency, Elizabeth seems not to recognize that in the process of running away from what she regards as problems—school, her family, a series of jobs from which she was fired—she has not yet established what she is running *towards*. What passes for Elizabeth's self-reliance in the first portion of the novel is in fact a fundamental childishness.

It is a problem that plagues virtually all of the characters in this novel, and it assumes a variety of guises. On the most obvious level, it is evident in infantile behavior. While shopping for a turkey, for example, Timothy coasts the grocery store aisles on the back of a shopping cart, an act of silliness which he attributes to a childhood lacking in visits to the market. Less publicly, in the privacy of her room Elizabeth, who favors the perennial summer-camp outfit of blue jeans, moccasins, and no make-up, reverts to a little girl: "She awoke here every morning feeling amazed all over again that she had finally become a grownup. Where to go and when to sleep and what to do with the day were hers to decide—or not to decide, which was even better" (33, 38).

In fact, of course, she hasn't "finally become a

THE CLOCK WINDER

grownup." With no sense of the possible consequences, Elizabeth blithely accepts all invitations. She imitates the sounds of inanimate objects, like bacon frying and trees growing. Locked in Timothy's room, she fires off elastic bands, chews gum, and randomly dials the telephone to harass total strangers. Were these discrete instances, they might, like Timothy's coasting on a shopping cart, be interpreted as charming, or as atypical acts due to stress. But instead Tyler is careful to posit them as in keeping with Elizabeth's childish impulses to drive recklessly without a license, to prefer traveling by car because "you can get off whenever you like" (49, 56), and to smoke Camels so as to antagonize her father's asthma. As a writer who relies heavily on charming eccentrics like Morgan Gower and Muriel Pritchett in her novels, Tyler is well aware that there is a fine line between an adult character's actions seeming charmingly childlike—or irritatingly childish. In the first portion of *The Clock Winder*, Elizabeth consistently crosses that line, as her seeming self-reliance is exposed as infantile selfishness.

The same selfishness is evident in the incapacity of virtually all the characters in this novel to communicate like adults. Matthew is well aware, for example, that "when Elizabeth answered questions with questions, it was no use trying to talk to her" (124, 139). More subtly, the Emerson children repeatedly elope without bothering to mention their marriages to anyone. Late in the novel, for instance, Peter and his "white-trash" bride

P.J. suddenly visit the Emersons after he's been away for three years. It is only when P.J. is asked her last name that the truth emerges that she, too, is now an Emerson. Had the question not arisen, Peter would never have volunteered the information. More dramatically, Tyler presents *The Clock Winder* partly in an epistolary format. The central portion of the novel (Chap. 7) consists entirely of letters in italics, from Andrew's brief, psychotic death threats to Elizabeth, to Matthew's whining, repetitious demands that she write to him and return his love. Models of non-communication, these letters—including those of Elizabeth, who gives "no more details than a fifth-grader might" (180, *201*)—accomplish nothing more than to get her multi-purpose drill mailed to her in Ellington, North Carolina, where she is living with her parents after Timothy's death. Perhaps most cogent of all, Mrs. Emerson writes "letters" to her children by dictaphone. As Anne G. Jones points out, a dictaphone, which by definition "never answers back," is the ideal symbol of Mrs. Emerson's "incessant self-involvement," a quality so strong that it even overrides her customary terror of mechanical devices. Like Ansel Green before her, she is essentially a "narcissistic" individual whose absolute self-absorption distorts her perception of herself and her family.[4] And in childishly insisting in her dictated letters that she is the perfect, non-meddling mother, Mrs. Emerson becomes the demanding drone who drives her family away.

THE CLOCK WINDER

That said, it would nonetheless be inaccurate to suggest that Mrs. Emerson is somehow solely responsible for the problems in this novel, that without her everyone would be refreshingly well-adjusted, independent, resilient, focused, happy—in short, adults enjoying a healthy dose of self-reliance. For once again Anne Tyler is arguing that one individual alone rarely is the sole culprit in another person's difficulties. Rather, it is the pressures and expectations foisted upon us by society at large, and acting through particular groups as social agents, that undermine the emergence of a strong sense of self and, in this novel, of self-reliance. More often than not in Tyler's novel, those agents are families, and usually parents rather than siblings. But as if deliberately to expand this paradigm of culpability, Tyler in *The Clock Winder* focuses for the first time on another such agent: organized religion.

If Mrs. Emerson seems the incarnation of maternal-figure as liability, then Elizabeth's father, John Abbott, performs the same function as a paternal figure. As his occupation (Baptist preacher) and surname (Abbott) would suggest, he is not just a biological father but also that more symbolic paternal figure, a minister; and in his interactions with his daughter he slides with alarming ease between his roles as biological parent and preacher, between being "Pop" and "Father" (151, *169*). The latter, pastoral role evidently is dearer to his identity than the parental. He "flinche[d]" when Elizabeth called him by his secular nickname (151, *169*), and she seems correct in believing that at times Rev. Abbott looks "haggard and beaten" because his family fails to "see him the way his congregation did" (150, *169*)—that is, as a smooth, all-wise showman on intimate terms with God. Further, he has never ceased being angry with Elizabeth for staying "glued to her seat in [a] revival tent" (150, *169*) many years before rather than announce publicly that she was "saved." No wonder Margaret Emerson, seeing him for the first time at Elizabeth's wedding to Dommie Whitehill, perceives him as "tall and handsome and frightening" (198, *220*). And no wonder either that Elizabeth, effectively hamstrung by his double authority as both father and minister, almost allows herself to be forced into marrying the milquetoast Dommie. Almost—but not quite. She knows only too well that her father wishes her to marry Dommie because it is a socially acceptable sign of maturity, and one especially expected of a preacher's daughter. Love simply is not at issue. And she also knows that it is his way of confirming publicly his personal control over his daughter's life, a motivation responsible for Anne Tyler's own admitted distrust of clergymen.[5] But she also knows that a primary reason he will not permit her to cancel her unwanted wedding at the last moment is that all the guests had already arrived, "and you owe them a wedding" (200, *223*). Society, acting through organized religion and in particular Rev. Abbott, was about to force her to make the biggest mistake of her life. Elizabeth seems always to have known, or at least sensed, the dubious motives underlying her father's cool, socially sanctioned exterior; but she had never been able to act on that realization by anything more constructive than running away or professing a fascination with reincarnation, something guaranteed to antagonize a good North Carolina Baptist.[6] It is to her credit that on the day of her aborted wedding, she is able fully to comprehend that Rev. Abbott's abdication of his roles as loving father and spiritual guide permits her to abdicate her roles as dutiful daughter and submissive lay person. She is finally able to act decisively. She leaves Dommie at the altar.

This jilting is, significantly, neither childish nor selfish. Rather it is arguably Elizabeth's first act of self-reliance in the novel, and it is made possible by three preparatory incidents. One is Margaret Emerson's recounting of her mother's forcing her to leave Jimmy Joe. A second is the suicide of Timothy. Up until he pulled the trigger, Elizabeth had been treating him and their relationship flippantly. It is a painful lesson for her, and she will put it to good use when Andrew threatens her later in the novel: "she had been through this before; she knew now that it was something to take seriously. Laughter tended to set explosions off" (252, 279). The realization that she must respond to the world as an adult, that she can no longer use jokes or non sequiturs to evade responsible actions, is initially what leads her to agree to that foremost adult act, getting married; but it also, significantly, is what subsequently enables her to refuse to go through with it.

The third preparatory incident that helps nurture the emergence of Elizabeth's self-reliance is her caring for a dying old man, Mr. Cunningham. Ironically, the job was obtained with the help of her father. It requires that she attend to the old man's physical needs, such as giving him water and handing him his false teeth, but more importantly it involves her interacting with him on a more emotional level. By reading to him and playing checkers with him, Elizabeth hopes to "[pin] his thoughts to the present moment, . . . to dig a groove too deep for his mind to escape from" (163, *182*). For although old age has taken its toll on his body, Mr. Cunningham's mind is intermittently sharp—sharp enough that he "could feel the skipped rhythms of his brain" (163, *182*). It is a terrifying realization for him, and as Elizabeth joins forces with him to preserve what's left of his mind, as she tries to assuage his fears, insecurities, and embarrassments, she comes to "care" for him empathetically more than physically. It is a sobering, serious matter, and under its pressure, her earlier, most irritating personality traits fade away: even Matthew observes that Elizabeth seems oddly "muffled" (172, *192*) after taking care of poor Mr. Cunningham.

At the same time, caring for him undermines Elizabeth's fear of assuming responsibility for others, something which is central to Tyler's interpretation of self-reliance. Early in the novel, Elizabeth tells Mrs. Emerson that she dislikes children, an emotion that seems less shocking and self-absorbed when she explains later that "I don't like people you can have so much effect on" (11, *14*). This fear is resurrected when she begins to care for Mr. Cunningham whom, she worries, is "sinking awfully *fast*": "Maybe, having found her to lean on, he had stopped making an effort. Maybe she was the worst thing in the world for him" (166, *185*). But of course he simply is dying of old age; and when he passes away a year and a half later, it seems natural rather than the result of Elizabeth's efforts. In the meantime, she knows that she had brought him great comfort in the last months of his life. Further, Mr. Cunningham had inadvertently zeroed in on the one thing that Elizabeth most feared. In paraphrasing a novel for him, she reports that one character had been asked to serve as sheriff of his Western town. "'I don't want the responsibility,' said Mr. Cunningham" (165, *184*), blurring his own identity with that of the character in the library book. "'It's too much. It's too much. It's too much'" (165, *185*). That, in brief, is Elizabeth's attitude towards everything in her life. But no one is asking her to be the sheriff of a town, or anything even remotely comparable to it. All she need do at this juncture is assume responsibility for Mr. Cunningham—and for herself. These responsibilities she can handle, and does; and her success with them paves the way for greater responsibilities involving other individuals, including her own children, George and Jenny.

Caring for old Mr. Cunningham further proves to be an ideal facilitator of the growth of Elizabeth's self-reliance by forcing her to reconsider her understanding of time. Clocks are, as noted, a central metaphor in this novel; and although critics have tended to overstate the services which this metaphor performs,[7] it nonetheless is adequate for Tyler's purposes. The clocks are, for example, emblematic of the life challenges which overwhelm Mrs. Emerson; she can deal with them even less than she can deal with garden shears, yellow pages, and license plates. But where the clocks begin to assume larger significance is the suggestion that to let them run down is tantamount to death. Mrs. Emerson, longing to synchronize their winding, considers letting them stop and then restarting them in unison, but "the symbolism involved—the tick, pause, tock, the pause and final tick of the grandfather clock in the hall, the first to go—made her so nervous that she abandoned the plan" (5, 8). (No protofeminist, Mrs. Emerson in 1960 cannot face the symbolic death of the "grandfather" clock, and she looks for approval from her husband, the one person able to fathom the system of clock-winding. He has, of course, been dead for three months when the novel opens.) The suggestion that the clocks are somehow alive is the corollary of the repeated statement that the human body is essentially a mechanism. Mrs. Emer-

THE CLOCK WINDER

son's heart specialist makes this explicit: "He kept comparing me to clocks and machines and worn-out cars, and the worst of it was that it all made sense. . . . All my parts are sealed in, air-tight. No replacements are possible." (69–70, 79) One of Elizabeth's jobs as handyman is, of course, to wind the clocks; but by declining to show her doing this, by treating it as no more monumental than her cleaning the gutters, Tyler places more emphasis on Elizabeth's function as the symbolic winder of all those running-down Emersons. She seems, as Mary Ellen Brooks argues, a "systematic source of energy": "Lives constantly wind down and then gain new momentum from Elizabeth's influence."[8] Though this is not entirely accurate—the dead Timothy and the still-gloomy Peter can hardly be said to receive momentum from anyone—it is true enough to confirm the importance of Elizabeth's role as a symbolic clock winder.

But what matters more is that clocks and people's lives have only minimal relation to time itself. Time moves steadily forward along an orderly continuum; however, people's perception of time, and the devices (such as clocks) which they use to measure it, are not so stable. Clocks and people can run down, can stop, can be overwound, can break—witness the number of references to insanity and death in this novel. Further, the hands of a clock can be literally and symbolically turned back. Mrs. Emerson tries desperately to do so, eschewing the "tweedy" sensible shoes of a grandmother (206, 229) in favor of painful spike heels, dyed

hair, and excessive make-up. But she feels that her efforts are working, that she is making a statement to her
ingrate children: "she had survived their desertion, she
had not become a broken old lady after all" (4, 7). Mr.
Cunningham, on the other hand, becomes younger, indeed childlike, through no effort of his own. His mind
wandering and regressing in his old age, he enjoys listening as Elizabeth reads him pulp Westerns; he speaks
of his little brother, dead at age two, whose name he
no longer remembers; and he announces proudly that
he will be "eighty-seven in November" (169, 189), much
as a child would nudge the calendar by claiming to be
"five-and-a-half" or "almost six." For Elizabeth, who begins the novel at age twenty-three (129, 145) but seems
to be about ten, the apparent chronological regressions
of those around her are thought-provoking:

Life might be a triangle, with adulthood as its apex; or
worse yet, a cycle of seasons, with childhood recurring
over and over like that cold rainy period in February.
Mr. Cunningham's hands were as small and curled as
a four-year-old's. His formless smile, directed at the
ceiling, had no more purpose than a baby's. (162, 181)

If, as the case of Mr. Cunningham suggests, there
really is no clear correlation between clock time and
maturity level, then mere aging does not guarantee the
emergence of any aspect of self, including self-reliance.

If that was what Elizabeth had been waiting for, if she had been killing time with a series of failed jobs and an unsuccessful college stint because she felt that maturity came automatically with the attainment of her legal majority, then she had only been fooling herself. It is possible, indeed it is necessary, to take the responsibility to nurture one's own self-reliance; and not long after Mr. Cunningham dies she does just that, first by taking a clerkship in a crafts shop, and then by doing something that would seem to be totally out of character for her: the former child-hater agrees to teach in a "children's school" (220, 244).

This startling change of heart was greatly facilitated by her successful caring for Mr. Cunningham, but its immediate impetus, and one perhaps too facile, is that she had had an epiphany while viewing a parade out the shop window. As she explains to Mrs. Emerson, she had never before realized how much is involved in raising a child:

"Isn't it amazing how hard people work to raise their children? Human beings are born so helpless, and stay helpless so long. For every grownup you see, you know there must have been at least one person who had the patience to lug them around, and feed them, and walk them nights and keep them out of danger for years and years, without a break. Teaching them how to fit into civilization . . ." (247, 274)

Though this is not qualitatively different from her earlier fear that she might adversely affect any child left in her care, her new attitude towards the situation is dramatically different:

"Then I thought, 'What am I doing up here, anyway? Up in this shop where I'm bored stiff? And never moving on into something else, for fear of some harm I might cause? You'd think I was some kind of special case,' I thought, 'but I'm not! I'm not! I'm like all the people I'm sitting here gawking at, and I might just as well stumble on out and join them!' So right that day I quit my job, and started casting about for new work. And found it—teaching crafts in a reform school." (247–48, 274)

It should come as no surprise to any reader of Anne Tyler's novels that what Elizabeth calls "crafts" is actually collage art. From Janie Rose Pike's tin-can tree to Drum Casey's "speaking out," creative individuals in the early Tyler try, with greater or lesser success, to incorporate the unconnected fragments of life—tin cans, popcorn, words—into wholes, to impose patterns of order on seeming disorder. Elizabeth Abbott tries to accomplish the same thing with household goods. Packing for her marriage to Dommie involves filling five cardboard boxes with "broken odds and ends," along with clock parts and burlap. "What are they *for?*' Margaret asked, and Elizabeth said, 'I may want to make something out of them'" (188, *210*). Apparently a dedicated artist and teacher, Elizabeth would certainly seem to have achieved a high level of self-reliance at this late stage of the novel: she supports herself financially (and Tyler is fully cognizant of the blunt need for money in the nurturance of the self[9]), while she is assuming responsibility for others, including a group of impressionable reform school inmates. Had *The Clock Winder* ended here, with Mrs. Emerson on the road to recovery and Elizabeth returning dutifully to care for her art students, then the novel would seem relatively tidy and complete. It would be a virtual *Bildungsroman*, tracing Elizabeth's emergence as an artist and as a self-reliant adult. But it does not end here. Tyler has Elizabeth leave her teaching job, move back in with the Emersons, marry Matthew, have two children, and reassume her old role of handyman—along with the new role, previously resisted, of housekeeper/cook. How can this be reconciled with *The Clock Winder* as a book of self-reliance?

The key to responding appropriately to this novel is, once again, Elizabeth's collage art. Unlike six-year-old Janie Rose, whose tree seems to have been a legitimate artistic rendering of spiritual truths, Elizabeth is not really an artist. Lacking a firm grasp of what collage art is or can do, she gropingly assembles household detritus and tries to teach art, without truly understanding it herself, to reform school girls. Her heart may be in the right place, but she cannot follow through with this on her own terms on a permanent basis.

UNDERSTANDING ANNE TYLER

So she moves back in with the Emersons. By not showing what Elizabeth did or thought during the several years of re-absorption into their world, Tyler seems to be suggesting that it was a matter less of struggle than surrender. Elizabeth is, once again, repairing the Emerson house, but she also is cooking, raising children, and protecting the Emersons, now including the contrite Andrew, from an onslaught of cicadas, those seventeen-year locusts that seem so determined to invade the household. The cicadas seem to have no relation to the pastoral landscape which Ralph Waldo Emerson had described so lovingly in yet another famous essay, "Nature." And that seems to be Anne Tyler's point. The pleasant world of Emerson's Concord during the New England "Indian Summer" before the Civil War has little or no relevance to Anne Tyler's Baltimore and North Carolina in the decades during and after the Vietnam War. Self-reliance is a wonderful notion. To attain it must be a major achievement. But the modern world is too complex and burdened to be amenable to true Emersonian self-reliance. Worse, as a quality it is confused too readily with the self-centered goals of the infamous "me generation"—one that, lacking Emerson's vocabulary, takes too much at face value his statements in "Self-Reliance" that "Whoso would be a man, must be a nonconformist" and that one should "write on the lintels of the door-post, *Whim.*"[10] Nonconformity and whimsy, as ends in themselves, are infantile; they have nothing to do with "self-reliance" as Emerson himself understood the term. True, Elizabeth Abbott had, thanks to harsh life experiences, begun to approach what Emerson would have regarded as self-reliance; but the complexities and burdens of life, plus her own limitations of character, finally had tripped her up as surely as the brambles had snagged Mrs. Emerson's stockings in her non-pastoral Baltimore backyard. She returns to the Emersons, where most of what she has achieved in terms of true self-reliance is diffused in a double loss of self: her surname Abbott becomes Emerson, while her given name Elizabeth is blurred into "Gillespie."

It was intended to be a sad ending. Several astute critics have realized this, including Wendy Lamb, who finds the Emersons' final "dependence on [Elizabeth] not only overwhelming but tragic," and Sara Blackburn, who notes that "the result smacks of a group of hurt and inept people propping one another up."[11] But more to the point, it is tragic for Elizabeth. Most critics, apparently noticing the reference to Elizabeth as a "broad golden madonna" (280, 309) without noticing the subsequent statement that she "looked like another child" (281, 311), blithely declare that the novel has a "happy" ending. Tyler herself disagrees:

"I think Elizabeth does herself irreparable damage in not going farther than she does, but on the other hand what she does is the best and happiest thing for her. I think of it as a sad ending, and I've been surprised that not everybody does."[12]

Perhaps reabsorption into the Emerson clan is the only mode of action available to someone like Elizabeth in an era when one can no longer light out for the territories to create a meaningful life safe from guilt, regret, and the entanglements, literal and figurative, that so striate Tyler's fictional landscape. *The Clock Winder* is thus a sorry commentary, one that exposes not the limitations of Emersonian thought, but rather the limitations of a world that can no longer respond meaningfully to his simple truths.

Notes

1. Alleen Pace Nilsen, for example, includes *The Clock Winder* on her "1972–73 Honor Listing" of books for younger readers. See "Books for Young Adults," *English Journal* 62 (December 1973): 1298.

2. Martin Levin, "New & Novel," *New York Times Book Review* (21 May 1972): 31. Barbara A. Bannon is one of the few critics to feel that "the story is beautifully structured." See her review in *Publishers Weekly* 201 (14 February 1972): 68.

3. Anne G. Jones, "Home at Last, and Homesick Again: The Ten Novels of Anne Tyler," *The Hollins Critic* 23 (April 1986): 4; and Mary Ellen Brooks, "Anne Tyler," in *The Dictionary of Literary Biography*, Vol. 6: *American Novelists Since World War II* (Detroit: Gale Research, 1980): 341.

4. Jones 5.

5. "It's not that I have anything against ministers, but that I'm particularly concerned with how much right anyone has to change someone, and ministers are people who feel they have that right." Quoted in Wendy Lamb, "An Interview with Anne Tyler," *Iowa Jour nal of Literary Studies* 3 (1981): 61.

6. It is unclear whether Elizabeth's interest in reincarnation is sincere, or simply another aspect of her determination to antagonize her father. Whatever the case, it may reflect, on some level, two other aspects of Emersonian thought: his interest in Eastern religions and rejection of conventional Christian practice, plus his related interest in the whole notion of cycles and circles. See in particular his essays entitled "The Divinity School Address" and "Circles."

7. Doris Betts, for example, argues that Tyler uses "assigned chapters in each [character's] point of view. These divisions make the novel's structure match its controlling metaphor since each character, even when synchronized with the others, will tick separately in the novel, just as many clocks tick in separate rooms in the Emerson household" ("The Fiction of Anne Tyler," *Southern Quarterly* 21 [Summer 1983]: 29). Though this sounds like an imaginative and useful technique, it actually is not evident in *The Clock Winder*. We do not see the story from each character's point of view (Andrew, Melissa, and Mary are notable omissions), while the unexpected, temporary emergence of certain characters (e.g., Timothy in Chap. 2, Margaret in Chap. 9, Peter in Chap. 13) renders the narrative more halting than rhythmic. Tyler will, however, use the technique of alternating points of view to good effect in her next novel, *Celestial Navigation*.

8. Brooks 341.

9. Part of Mrs. Emerson's infantile need to be taken care of and her incapacity to make decisions seem due a lifetime spent in the control of financially powerful males. "She was not a stupid woman, but she was used to being taken care of. She had passed almost without a jolt from the hands of her [wealthy] father to the hands of her husband . . ." (5–6, *8*). Mr. Emerson's finances had helped to render

his wife simultaneously safe and childlike: "Oh, where was her husband, with his desk-size checkbook and his bills on a spindle and his wallet that unfolded so smartly whenever she was sad, offering her money for a new outfit or a trip to Washington?" (8, 10). Like Evie Decker in *A Slipping-Down Life,* Elizabeth Abbott never seems more independent and self-assured than when she has a "real" job, however modest it may be, while Mrs. Emerson's station in life had prevented her from taking advantage of the strength to be gained from having an income of her own. By being so aware of the power of money and the need for meaningful work if a person (and in particular a woman) is to acquire a firm sense of self, and by avoiding too-easy, "feel good" happy endings, Tyler emerges as much more of a feminist and realist than many commentators have been wont to admit.

10. "Self-Reliance," in *Selections from Ralph Waldo Emerson: An Organic Anthology,* ed. Stephen E. Whicher (Boston: Houghton Mifflin, 1960): 149, 150.

11. Lamb 59; and Sara Blackburn, [rev. of *The Clock Winder*], *Washington Post Book World* (14 May 1972): 13.

12. Quoted in Clifford A. Ridley, "Anne Tyler: A Sense of Reticence Balanced by 'Oh, Well, Why Not?.'" *National Observer* 11 (22 July 1972): 23. Tyler's ambivalence towards the final image of Elizabeth Abbott, her belief that she has done "damage" to herself while still being as happy as it is possible for her to be, may suggest that Elizabeth has something in common with Tyler herself. Both, after all, seem torn between nurturing a true sense of personal selfhood, and caring for a home and children. Though her two daughters are now grown, Tyler at the time she wrote *The Clock Winder* in the early 1970s was having difficulty reconciling her roles as housewife/mother and professional novelist. (See, for example, her essay "Still Just Writing," in Janet Sternburg, ed., *The Writer on Her Work* [New York: Norton, 1980]: 3–16.) Further, Tyler has admitted that she, like Elizabeth, had gone through a phase of cultivating nonconformity as an end in itself: " 'There was a period in my life, starting at 17 or 18, when I seemed determined to do whatever seemed the most contrary thing. . . .

THE CLOCK WINDER

When I decided to get married, for instance, I remember thinking "Oh, well, why not?" Fortunately, of course'—a smile—'it worked out'" (Ridley 23). But Tyler is careful to emphasize that Elizabeth is not a portrait of herself when younger: "'I'm getting a little more and more willing to expose more of myself with each book. There's more of *me* in *The Clock Winder*—not autobiography, but more that I feel'" (Ridley 23). There will be even more of what Tyler "feels" in her next novel, *Celestial Navigation*.

CHAPTER FIVE

Celestial Navigation

The centrality of *Celestial Navigation* (1974) in Anne Tyler's literary canon would seem confirmed by two apparently incompatible observations: she found it extremely difficult, even painful to write—and once finished, it proved to be her favorite novel.[1] The difficulty of its composition had little to do with the high degree of technical and stylistic experimentation involved. A novel which, as Mary Ellen Brooks writes, "marks a turning point in [Tyler's] stylistic maturity," *Celestial Navigation* is characterized by an "intricate design"[2] featuring five distinct points of view and covering a thirteen-year period. Perhaps encouraged by her success with the less sophisticated use of multiple narration and sequentially blocked time in *The Clock Winder*, Tyler in this novel opts to present the story of her artist-protagonist, Jeremy Pauling, in a fashion of suitable complexity for this complex man. She also uses, with unprecedented skill, such tropes as the "ocean" of real life and the "island" of creative endeavor in ways that seem to arise naturally out of the story. By far the most tightly

CELESTIAL NAVIGATION

controlled of her first five novels, *Celestial Navigation* is particularly noteworthy for the open recognition of unresolved tensions and difficulties at its core: situations that might have seemed vague or contradictory in earlier novels—including the notion that such "good" things as maternal behavior, personal independence, and creativity may be liabilities under certain circumstances—are here exploited for their ambiguity and irony.

These are all sure touches, of the sort one finds in the work of a mature professional novelist, and Tyler seems to have found the process of working through them to be an interesting challenge, not a source of dismay. The difficulties involved in the creation of *Celestial Navigation* thus were not technical or stylistic, but personal. At the time she began work on it, Tyler was closing a particular chapter in her life. Both daughters had begun grade school, and Tyler was faced with a circumstance known to have incapacitated lesser writers: she had ample free time in which to work—and no more excuses for failing to work at full capacity. Psychologically, she was overwhelmed. Constantly "fighting the urge to remain in retreat even though the children had started school," Tyler admits that her work on *Celestial Navigation* "made me sick all the way through." She even admits to indulging in the kinds of evasion tactics familiar to anyone who writes: "I'd go into my study and think, I really need shoelaces. Then I'd get in the car and drive five miles to get those shoelaces."[3]

UNDERSTANDING ANNE TYLER

No wonder *Celestial Navigation* took two years to complete.

But the other personal difficulties at the heart of the creation of this novel were more elusive than this. Margaret Morganroth Gullette argues, for example, that the novel shows Tyler working through the final stages of a fear of motherhood.[4] It is akin, one may surmise, to Elizabeth Abbott's fear of making a mistake that might ruin an innocent child for life. Even more subtle, the difficulties Anne Tyler experienced while working on *Celestial Navigation* seem to have stemmed from the realization that in writing about Jeremy Pauling—in exposing this artist's insecurities, behavioral aberrations, eccentric work habits, and personality problems—she was hitting rather too close to home. Raised in a family that actively encouraged creative activity, accustomed to doodling characters before writing about them, and reportedly still fantasizing about becoming a book illustrator someday,[5] Anne Tyler identifies quite strongly with individuals in the fine arts. Though it would be inaccurate to argue that Tyler was the prototype for Jeremy Pauling—that distinction belongs to an ex-mental patient whom she had known slightly[6]—it seems nonetheless true that Jeremy and his creator have a good deal in common.

The components of that commonality are varied and far-ranging, and they would be evident to anyone familiar with Anne Tyler's various interviews and personal statements. Both Tyler and Jeremy, for example, lose touch with domestic reality when creating. Jeremy's "breakfast was other people's lunch," and he usually eats "whatever took the least trouble—a box of day-old doughnuts or a can of cold soup" (102, *115*). Though Tyler's case seems not so extreme, she admitted frankly in 1977 that "my family can always tell when I'm well into a novel because the meals get very crummy."[7] Likewise, both live in terror of physical impairment of particular kinds. Jeremy, for example, regards color blindness as "the worst affliction he could imagine next to blindness itself" (109, *123*). Working entirely in long-hand using Parker ballpoint pens (two dozen refills are kept nearby lest the company go bankrupt and leave her unable to finish her book[8]), Tyler worries "'What if I got arthritis? It's my second greatest fear. Next to going blind, because it matters very much how the words look on the page.'" Further, Tyler never types because "then I wouldn't hear my characters' voices."[9] Realizing fully well how bizarre it would sound to a non-creative individual, she nonetheless admits that she regards her characters as actual people who tell her their stories, usually between 2:00 and 4:00 A.M.[10] Tyler's books thus are, in a way, not written by her, and she confesses to "feeling like an imposter" when she autographs one of her novels.[11] In a less dramatic way, the hearing of voices is a phenomenon familiar even to Jeremy, though he works in a non-verbal medium:

Imaginary voices murmured in his ear. Scraps of conversation floated past. He was used to that when he was working. Some phrases had recurred for most of his life, although they had no significance for him. "At least he is a *gentle* man," one voice was sure to say. He had no idea why. (80, *90–91*)

In addition, both Jeremy and Tyler listen for a "click" that confirms they are on the right creative track. Jeremy dreams of working on his art projects, waiting for the "click in his head to tell him he was finally right" (225, *250*), while Tyler—who meticulously orders plot lines, character traits, symbols, even details of clothing on her elaborate system of index cards—always begins a new novel by sifting through them. When "a little click" goes off in her head, she sets the card aside. The resultant pile of index cards forms the nucleus of the new book.[12]

But shared fears and rituals (what Tyler terms her "magic spells"[13]) are only the most blatant parallels between Jeremy Pauling and his creator. More important are the less obvious parallels involving attitudes and relationships. Anne Tyler remarked in 1981, for example, that although prior to beginning her career she was outgoing ("Before I was married, it seemed I was always on a train"), the subsequent commitment to a writing career had made her "increasingly closed down, self-protective," not just in the sense of refusing to give lectures or attend PTA meetings, but on the more basic level of avoiding contact with the outside world.[14] She believes strongly that "creating Jeremy was a way of investigating her own 'tendency to turn more and more inward,'" even to the point of dreading to make telephone calls.[15]

Though Jeremy embodies hyperbolically Tyler's tendency towards reclusiveness—unlike him, she would not feel "flattened and defeated" by the prospect of a two-minute call to the gas company (70, *86*)—they do seem to share a tendency to observe the world from a distance, whether literally (Jeremy, of course, looks through two "frames," the window of his third-floor studio and the screen of his television set) or figuratively, through what Tyler terms a "setting-apart situation":[16]

"I guess I work from a combination of curiosity and distance," says Tyler. "It seems to me often that I'm sort of looking from a window at something at a great distance and wondering what it is. But I'm not willing to actually go into it. I would rather sit behind the windowsill and write about it. So all my curiosity has to be answered within myself instead of by crossing the street and asking what's going on."[17]

However necessary this distance may be, both as a means of giving the artist/writer the objectivity essential to his personal vision and as a guarantee of the physical privacy required to work in peace, it pulls the creative individual away from the outside world which both in-

UNDERSTANDING ANNE TYLER

spires his work and which, at some point, evaluates his vision, be it through criticism or sales. The artist, by definition original and independent, is thus an intensely private individual forced to exist in a tenuous, even adversarial relationship with a public that may not understand or accept either his personal vision or the conditions under which he works. So a problem arises: where does one draw the line between an artist's being "private" and "anti-social," between his being "offbeat"—and insane? The lines between these categories are indistinct. And though they are labels imposed by a society that cannot itself always agree on their precise nature, they nonetheless are real mind-sets that are potentially dangerous to the creative individual. It is a tragic price to pay for being an artist, and one that Tyler explores at length in *Celestial Navigation*.

Having no physical niche in his world beyond the remote studio in which he works or gazes out the window and the living room in which he watches television, Jeremy Pauling is very much the artist-as-eccentric, and perhaps something worse. Because of the uncertainty surrounding his emotional stability, it is essential that he be considered from as many angles as possible. Hence the experimentation with point of view in *Celestial Navigation*, a device as essential to this novel as it is to Faulkner's *As I Lay Dying* (1930). The story opens with a chapter presented from the point of view of Jeremy's older sister, Amanda, a spinster schoolteacher whose life-long sense of being unloved has twisted her into a cold and judgmental monster of the self-reliance Tyler had explored in *The Clock Winder*. She has no patience with her brother's passivity and reclusiveness, insisting that he should "jerk" [him]self up by [his] own bootstraps, it's all a matter of will" (30, *36*). It is evident throughout her chapter that Amanda sees a superficial aspect of Jeremy's situation, his reclusiveness, without perceiving either its seriousness, its source, its relationship to his work, or the best way to resolve it—if, indeed, it can or should be resolved.

Whereas Amanda's point of view is limited and static, Mary Tell's point of view shifts dramatically, depending upon the degree of her intimacy with Jeremy. In her first chapter (number three), she regards him simply as her landlord. Too caught up in her own relationships with John Harris ("the cigarette-ad man" [88, *100*]), her estranged husband Guy, and her daughter Darcy, Mary initially sees only Jeremy's physical surface: "The man who owns this boarding house is very odd, and at first I was afraid of him. He reminded me of a slug. . . . But when I had been here longer I saw that he wouldn't harm a fly, and now I let him talk with Darcy even when I am in another part of the house." (53, 61). At this early stage, she regards his art projects as "kaleidoscope things" (54, *61*), and she is interested in his career only to the extent that Jeremy lets Darcy cut and paste in his studio. When Tyler next provides a chapter from Mary's point of view (number seven), she has already become Jeremy's common-law wife, borne him five children, and decided to leave him. Under the pressure of this intimacy and emotional turmoil, Mary's perception of Jeremy is complex, both understandably bitter and surprisingly sympathetic. Angry at his failure to comprehend that the children required his personal input, that "you don't just tie off their little navel cords and toss them on their way like balloons" (181, 202), Mary nonetheless recognizes that in their marriage she was always "the interrupter, the overwhelmer" (181, 201) who disrupted Jeremy's work and privacy to an intolerable degree. Unable to stop loving him, Mary feels, like Ellen Hawkes before her, that "if he said a single word to keep me with him, I would gladly stay forever" (174, 194). Though Mary is a perceptive woman, she evidently is not perceptive enough to realize the impossibility of Jeremy ever fulfilling that condition. Able to express himself only through his art, he of course says nothing.

The two chapters presented from the point of view of Miss Mildred Vinton are just as sympathetic, and decidedly more perceptive. A long-term boarder who has shared a house with Jeremy for years, Miss Vinton is also an elderly person who has had enough first-hand experience with life to accept Jeremy's limits and foibles. She can appreciate fully Jeremy's desire for solitude, since for years her own fantasy was to "be reading a book alone in my room, and no one would ever, ever interrupt me" (123, 139). Believing Jeremy to be "a very special man," "a genius" (128, 143), she nevertheless recognizes that his increasing personal isolation might, ironically, isolate even his art: "the better his pieces get the more he shuts them away from us. Someday, I believe, Jeremy is going to be a very famous man, but it is possible that no one will be allowed to see his work at all by then, not even strangers in museums" (119, 134). Even so, she feels that there is much to admire about Jeremy, including his willingness (Mary's complaints notwithstanding) to respond to his children. As Miss Vinton reports, when Darcy portrayed a flower in her school play, Jeremy walked seven blocks to see her: "I admired him for that. There are other kinds of heroes than the ones who swim through burning oil" (127, 143).

Miss Vinton's understanding of and admiration for Jeremy effectively counters the bitter, condemnatory analysis offered by his estranged sister Amanda, while qualifying the complaints of Mary—someone whom Miss Vinton finds well-meaning but limited in her capacity to deal with others. In contrast, probably the least accurate appraisal of Jeremy is that of Olivia, the tie-dyed teen whose brief stay in the boarding house and limited knowledge of life impart a self-serving edge to her adoration of Jeremy. Maintaining that "I have the deepest respect for artists," Olivia babbles mindless appraisals of Jeremy's work: " 'It's got a good flow to it,' I said. To tell the truth I didn't have the vaguest idea what comments were required, but I was going to learn" (203, 226–27). She also keeps him supplied with granola and homemade peanut butter that Miss Vinton realizes Jeremy would never eat, all the while "hoping to be defined" (204, *228*) by an intimate relationship with a Real Artist. She yearns to cement a relationship that exists only in her head, nudging her would-be lover/mentor with "'Oh, Jeremy, don't you just love talking this way? . . . Don't we get along beautifully together?'" (208, *232*). She even imagines that they are characters in a motion picture: "I was only a side character but powerful, a major influence, and the last scene would show me holding his head as he died. Some major transformation in his art would be dated from the time he met me." (206, *230*).

Jeremy, of course, does not realize he is part of Olivia's fantasy world, so his reactions are, in Olivia's eyes, inappropriate. For example, when his eyes open wide and his mouth falls open, Olivia remarks that "I wasn't expecting so much attention so suddenly" (203, *227*)—but what she mistakes for "attention" is actually the prelude to a fit of vomiting triggered by his smoking a cigarette. By the time Olivia hitchhikes her way out of the novel, she has been jolted into a somewhat clearer perspective both of Jeremy's love for his family (as evidenced by the cross-section of a people-less dollhouse he creates) and of his emotional problems ("Only crazy people smile like that" [222, *247*]). Jeremy is neither the stereotypical movie version of a painter nor the kind of individual capable of imparting an identity to anyone else. A "doughy" man with "white, white skin"

CELESTIAL NAVIGATION

(11, 74, *14, 84*) and eyes that seem those of an albino (11, *15*), Jeremy has little color or substance of his own. Most of it, Tyler would seem to suggest, has been channelled into his art.

Whether Jeremy truly is "crazy" for having his life so totally immersed in his art depends upon one's definition of insanity, coupled with the evidence presented in the six chapters narrated by Amanda, Mary, Miss Vinton, and Olivia. Another important source of input is the four remaining chapters, presented from what ordinarily would be the least reliable point of view of all: that of Jeremy himself. Whereas the other chapters are presented in the first-person ("I"), Jeremy's use the third ("he"), a technique which initially would seem to confirm that he is suffering from some sort of psychic split and, hence, would be unreliable as a source of any information, particularly about himself. But it seems more accurate to say that Jeremy simply is acting on his artist's compulsion to stand apart, to study and evaluate people. In this case the subject of his scrutiny happens to be himself, and he does indeed appear to have a remarkably astute understanding of his life, work, and environment. To be sure, he does tend to respond to the world on a visual level ("Here is Mrs. Jarrett . . . How gently the planes of her face meet, each meeting prepared for by those little powdery pouches" [42, *49*]), and he often seems out of touch with reality: "Jeremy watched the bacon crinkling in slow motion. He saw wisps of gray smoke rise toward the ceiling, blurring the kitchen. How long had he been here? Was it for lunch or for supper? Had he eaten yet?" (42, *49*). But since the former seems to be the automatic response of one trained in the fine arts, and since the latter reflects the absentmindedness of one engrossed in complex projects, they are not necessarily indicative of mental illness. Perhaps more to the point, Jeremy is not so out of touch that he cannot make realistic, even harsh appraisals of those around him, and even himself. He is painfully aware of his ignorance of the unwritten rules of courtship, offering his boarder Mary Tell a bouquet of weeds and forgetting to give her the crumpled box of chocolates which he had ventured out to buy for her. Later, when they are married, he is angry at her for assuming that he knows nothing of what occurs beyond his studio: "he had kept up with things. He knew what was going on in the world. Mary underestimated him" (145, *162*). And when finally she leaves him, children in tow, he goes after them on a city bus, refusing to give in to his impulse to run back. But for all Jeremy's emotionally-healthy insight into himself and his world, two glaring, related facts remain: he is agoraphobic, and he cannot function without a mother-figure. Both elements embody the novel's theme that "good" things can, under pressure from reality, be rendered serious liabilities.

Jeremy's agoraphobia is made explicit from the very opening of *Celestial Navigation*. He finds it virtually impossible to walk out his front door; even so, when smitten by Mary Tell, he impulsively accompanies her and

Darcy to a grocery two blocks from home. The ordeal proves too much for him: "Dread rose in him like a flood in a basement . . . Nausea came swooping over him, and he buckled at the knees and slid downward until he was seated flat on the sidewalk with his feet sticking out in front of him." (98, *110*). Though she "didn't know the condition 'agoraphobia' existed" when she wrote the book, Tyler is depicting a classic case: Jeremy's absolute terror of the street itself, his delusive conviction that "a mean-eyed woman watched him from her front stoop," his desperate strategy to "pretend this [street] is only a corridor leading off from the vestibule. Pretend it is just an unusually long room. It will all be over in a while" (96, *108–09*). But what is more important than the agoraphobia itself is the fact that it is a psychotic manifestation of his non-psychotic recognition of his need for personal space, both as a person and an artist.

Acutely conscious of the importance of personal space—an awareness shared by Miss Vinton, who contends that "our whole society would be better off living in boarding houses," with each person assigned his own room with a locked door (125, *141*)—Jeremy is literally in his element in his third-floor studio. He can see out his window on the world, but no one can see in—an arrangement similar to watching television. Further, he knows exactly where everything is in his studio, right down to the brushes. Despite the clutter and filth, it has an inherent order which Mary, bringing his lunch, cannot detect: "Every time she set a dish down she had to move something of his out of the way. A glue bucket was pushed aside, a paintbrush was laid across the top of it (not where it belonged)" (159, *177*). Also, he can use his studio as a secure base for raids on other parts of the house, including, ironically, the personal space of his own children, whose bedrooms are treasure troves of toys and clothing to be incorporated into his art projects. In his studio Jeremy can work, think, sleep, eat—in a word, live.

So perfect is the studio as his personal living and working space that Jeremy fantasizes about having the ultimate studio, "a small, bare, whitewashed cubicle, possibly in a desert" (152, *170*). Several things are striking about this fantasy studio. For one, it sounds suspiciously like Anne Tyler's own austere studio in her Baltimore home: "there is only one room I can work in—a stern white cubicle. Most of the pictures on its walls (I realized one day) have to do with isolation: uninhabited houses, deserted courtrooms, stark old men staring into space."[18] To Tyler, the "cubicle" seems a source of protection, of reassuring security, the physical manifestation of the "partitions" that she admits to erecting "around the part of me that writes." She has learned "how to close the door on it when ordinary life intervenes, how to close the door on ordinary life when it's time to start writing again."[19] Jeremy, of course, puts a locked door on his studio once his children begin to invade it; but what locks them out also locks him inside, and the "cubicle" thus becomes a barren prison, one that cuts the inhabitant off from life even as it protects him. Hence the importance of the fantasy studio being placed in a "desert." By definition, a desert lacks two things: other people, and water. For Jeremy, these have merged in the double trope of oceans and islands.

This trope is established early, and Tyler develops it consistently until virtually the last page of *Celestial Navigation*. Watching television in the living room, a place dangerously close to the front door and hence to the exterior world, Jeremy "was conscious of particles of dark floating between people, some deep substance in which they all swam, intent upon keeping their heads free, their chins straining upward" (46, *53*). And when he accompanies Mary to the market, he is in terror lest he be "marooned" next to Perry's grocery, so awful is the prospect of crossing the street to return home: "He imagined himself dipping the toe of one shoe into the street, then drawing it out and turning away, unable to cross" (97, *109–10*). To his credit, Jeremy realizes that this is a problem, and one that cannot be resolved without outside help. He decides to wed Mary precisely because "maybe, given time, he could follow [her] all the way off his island" (92, *104*). Strong, organized, and reassuringly large-knuckled, the sturdy Mary could, he believes, be the ideal companion for him, someone who could offer more dimension to his life than his increasingly inward-turning art. To a certain extent, his surmise is correct: once his common-law marriage is established, he does venture out more into the neighborhood, and his art does become richer, more dimensional, more textured. But there is another, more counterproductive motive behind his marriage about which Jeremy seems not to have been fully conscious: the artist in him is clamoring not for a wife and partner, but for a mother/manager.

Mary Tell is already a mother by the time she arrives at the Pauling boarding house, an arrival that comes shortly after the death of Jeremy's own mother, Wilma. He had not taken well her demise. Though it had upset Jeremy to be forced to invade her own personal space (closets, bureau drawers) to locate clothing suitable for her burial, what seems to have upset him more is that her death occurred on the stairs while they were climbing to his studio. He had heard her collapse with "a soft sound like old clothes dropping" (43, 50), but had simply continued on to his studio, effectively denying her death. Even the funeral arrangements, all made by the dreaded telephone, did not require him to deal directly with her corpse. When shortly after the funeral Mary arrived, she moved into Mrs. Pauling's old room; and when she agreed to be Jeremy's common-law wife, he moved into his mother's room with her. Though they eventually have five children together, Jeremy and Mary hardly come across as husband and wife—a non-relationship confirmed by their non-marriage. Indeed, Jeremy cannot help but feel that "Mary's pregnancies appeared to be entirely her own undertakings" (141, 158): his children bear no physical resemblance to him, they never call him "Daddy" (228, *254*), and they boldly venture forth into those terrifying Baltimore streets. Perennially attired in a madonna-blue maternity dress, Mary firmly believes that "motherhood is what I was made for" (61, *69*), and it is to her role as a mother-figure that the artist in Jeremy seems to have responded. His recognition of her as a potential mother, not so much for his biological children as for himself, is what triggers their relationship. When Jeremy collapses on the sidewalk in agoraphobic terror in front of Perry's, he impulsively proposes marriage to Mary from an angle that makes him seem like a small boy: "Her sandals were the largest thing about her. The hem of her skirt was so close he could see the stitches, he saw the underside of her bosom and the triangle below her jaw. 'Will you marry me?' he asked her" (98, *111*). Still legally wed to Guy, she cannot accept his offer, "but I'll see you home and into bed" (98, *111*). These ambiguous words are the kind that a woman would make to her lover—or to her little boy. And shortly thereafter, they do leave for home: "Like a child he let himself be led home while all his attention was directed toward the [cinnamon graham] cracker" (99, *112*) that she had given Jeremy to comfort him after his collapse.

For a while Jeremy is contented to be taken care of by Mary, his Earth Motherly manager. She deals with pesky quotidian realities, cleaning the mold out of the refrigerator, making Jeremy's lunch, and storing sneakers and laundry detergent by the barrel in their packed

UNDERSTANDING ANNE TYLER

basement. She even deals with the unappealing commercial aspects of his art career, making shopping runs to the art supply store and working closely with dealer Brian O'Donnell regarding the display and selling of Jeremy's artwork—the kinds of commercial concerns that Tyler finds most distasteful about her own career.[20]

But though a part of Jeremy needs and wants to have Mary as his mother/manager, another part of him resents it, and to an increasing degree. He is angered, for example, that she tries to calm him down at Brian's gallery, not with a cracker but a maternal kiss: "'There now,' she said. But she only troubled him more. Was it expected of him also that he would stand here being kissed like a child? He wiped away the damp equal-sign left by her lips, and he pulled his coat more tightly around him and trudged off toward the car" (148, *165*). The situation worsens when, hoping to spare him the distress and lost time of witnessing the birth of Edward, she does not awaken him to take her to to the hospital. In her effort to protect and comfort Jeremy as a kind mother would, Mary inadvertently sends him the emasculating message that he is neither needed nor wanted as a husband and father, roles that he had steadily tried to embrace as their relationship continued.

The final blow comes at Brian's cabin, where Mary moves in a kind of feminist rendering of Thoreau's stay at Walden Pond. Though the cabin is actually a filthy, unheated shack and the pond is a brackish river, Mary is understandably proud of her newfound ability to care for herself and her children without the support or presence of any man. But though she cherishes her new feelings of competence and independence, she cannot perceive that Jeremy, too, wants to be treated like an adult. Only reluctantly does she let him help her to winterize her cabin, and she will not entrust their children to him as he rows out to air the sails of Brian's boat. The scene closes with Jeremy alone on the sailboat as it "scudded around its mooring in wider and faster circles." He sees his gray golf cap "bob off across a wave and grow dark and heavy and finally sink" (247, *274*).

The sinking of a hat traditionally is a symbol of death; and certainly the "new" Jeremy—more satisfied than he had realized with being a husband and father, but unable to express it—has effectively died with the emergence of the "new" Mary and the loss of his children. But the idea that he has lost whatever growth he has made is conveyed even more effectively by the moored sailboat scudding in circles. Moving steadily but making no progress, the boat confirms the complexity of the idea of "celestial navigation."

The term itself, well known to sailors and pilots, involves the yoking of two motifs central to this novel. The word "celestial" refers of course to stars. Stars are far from earth, as indeed is Jeremy in his third-story studio and, more abstractly, in his tendency to respond to life "at a distance" (129, *145*). The distance between himself and the *"earthbound"* Mary (201, *225*) is so immense that he cannot make permanent, meaningful contact with her or their children, however much a part of him may yearn to do so. At the same time, the idea of Jeremy's "celestial" (i.e., "heavenly") orientation is in keeping with the ancient notion that painters, poets, and singers are closer to God than are mere mortals. In effect, artistic individuals were traditionally regarded as spokespersons for supernatural forces, visionaries who enabled mankind to see the world from a higher, and hopefully more objective, perspective. This rather poetic interpretation of Jeremy's seeming otherworldliness is expressed by Miss Vinton, who feels that the navigation by which he sails as an artist "is far more celestial" than the ordinary stars by which Brian steers his boat (130, *146*).

Further, stars are immensely old, and they theoretically will continue to exist for billions of years. This implication of timelessness is very much in keeping with Tyler's presentation of Jeremy. Disregarding for a moment his apparent social retardation, one sees that Jeremy genuinely enjoys such childish pursuits as watching *Sesame Street* (213, *237*)—and yet he is old, many years Mary's senior, and certainly old enough to have served in World War II (193, *215*). The uncertainty of his age underscores his role as artist. A fine piece of art will, of course, seem as fresh as today; but it will have meaning and impact centuries hence, and it taps into ideas and tropes as ancient as man himself. The vapid Olivia unwittingly touches upon this when she tries unsuccessfully to categorize Jeremy. He feels a strong kinship to the cave artist, who drew pictures "to comfort himself" (208, *232*). But Olivia surmises that he may in fact be a Martian, a being she feels does not come from Mars: "How come we think they're from another planet? They're from *our* planet, Jeremy, twenty centuries in the future." And she asks him an unsettling question: "Do you know what time you're from? Do you? *Think* Jeremy." Rather than face the answer, Jeremy evades Olivia with "I wish you could learn how to make waffles" (215–16, *240–41*). Unable or unwilling to acknowledge that he is, as an artist, as timeless as the stars—and thus, by implication, cut off from the possibility of pursuing such time-locked roles as adult or father—he yearns "to find just one heroic undertaking that he could aim his life toward" (227, *252*). Like ancient mariners or futuristic astronauts, Jeremy wants to do something "heroic," something more concrete than the fantasy rescue of Mary Tell from the "sweatshop" of knitting argyle socks (105, *119*). The only "heroic" thing available to him is to aim high as an artist.

Sailors would, of course, aim their boats either at particular stars (such as the North Star) or at particular constellations; and as stars in patterns or designs, constellations convey even more vividly the idea of the artist as a celestial navigator. As an artist, Jeremy looks actively for patterns and meanings: "He makes pictures the way other men make maps—setting down the few fixed points that he knows, hoping they will guide him as he goes floating through this unfamiliar planet" (129, *145*). "Hoping" is, unfortunately, the operative word. As he assembles bits and pieces of his life—baby spoons, plastic toy bananas—in his increasingly complex and multi-dimensional collages, he is working not so much from a comprehensive vision as towards one. He too readily is caught up in the distracting details of here and now, and in doing so fails to see the larger picture. It has been a lifelong problem: "When Jeremy was seven he made a drawing of his mother's parlor. Long slashes for walls and ceiling, curves for furniture, a single scribbled rose denoting the wallpaper pattern. And then, on the baseboard, a tiny electrical socket, its right angles crisp and precise, its screws neatly bisected by microscopic slits." However charming it may be, the picture points to a fundamental problem: "That was the way his vision functioned: only in detail. Piece by piece. He had tried looking at the whole of things but it never worked out" (38–39, *45*). Things had not improved with marriage. Too overwhelmed by the day-to-day details of raising children, the interruptions and runny noses, Jeremy failed to see the larger picture: the long-term impact of his family on his own life. Aiming for one star, one constellation, he could not see the larger pattern of the cosmos.

The second half of the term "celestial navigation" underscores this. The word "navigation" has as its root the Latin word for ship (*navis*). It specifically means, therefore, to travel on water. Jeremy, of course, is terrified of the murky ocean of reality surrounding him. Those stars, evident only in darkness, would seem to be the ideal agents for guiding him through these terrifying waters. But stars are effective only up to a degree. As the fixed points on maps, they can, unfortunately, be misread, as surely as Jeremy might misread the maps of the Baltimore bus routes and "never get home again" (230, 255). But more seriously, these stars only seem to form patterns. Most stars in a given constellation are nowhere near each other. The designs they form are simply constructs of the human eye and the human imagination, neither of which, to be sure, is infallible. Thus to navigate by stars is to run the risks of misreading the fixed points and becoming lost or, what is worse, of using as one's guide something that is no guide at all.[21] Those stars may simply send the celestial navigator on a wild goose chase, made more painful by the fact that he may not be able to determine a better guide for action. One such navigator is Jeremy. Separated from his family feebling tooting their whistles on the shore, he can only go in circles. He returns home to revert to his old, pre-Mary ways, with Miss Vinton installed as the new motherly manager.

It is not, as Jay L. Halio argues, "a defect in the novel" that "we never see the stars [Jeremy] navigates by,"[22] for it seems to be Tyler's point that only he is capable of seeing them—if, in fact, they even exist. Nor is Tyler "too oblique": the answers to the questions raised by Alan Pryce-Jones—"Who in her celestial navigation is sailing, and whither? Are we to think the stars always contrary?"[23]—are implicit in her portrait of Jeremy. What seems to be a far more important question is the implications of the novel concluding in a way Tyler had not intended. It was to have been a happy ending, but it twisted itself into something quite different:

"I've had several angry letters and calls from people who've wanted a happy ending for *Celestial Navigation*—they wanted the man and woman to stay together. All along I wanted that ending, too, and I was sure I'd be able to work out a way. I kept pushing toward it, but that writing felt wooden: my sentences were jerky when I looked back at them. In a way I felt I was trying to cover up a lie, and then I thought, I may as well tell the truth: the woman leaves the man. The problem in *Celestial Navigation* was that those characters were two absolutely separate people, and they couldn't possibly have stayed together."[24]

But if Jeremy's story is a sad one, Anne Tyler's is not. Unlike Jeremy, she has been able to set up her austere white cubicle within the larger confines of a house containing a husband and children. She has been able to work her way through to a conviction that family commitments could not only be accommodated with a creative career, but could actually enhance it: "It seems to me that since I've had children, I've grown richer and deeper. They may have slowed down my writing for a while, but when I did write, I had more of a self to speak from."[25] Though Jeremy had begun to grope his way towards this realization of the symbiosis of life and art— his "pieces," after all, had begun to gain both dimension and texture, while his visit to the bus stop confirmed that real "humanity was far more complex and untidy and depressing" than his art had suggested (230, 256)[26]—he could not make the final leap necessary actually to marry Mary legally and to commit himself permanently to the very forces that were enriching his outlook and art. Artists supposedly tend to be self-destructive, but few more than Jeremy Pauling, unhitching his wagon from the right star.

Notes

1. "Tyler says that she is 'very, very fond of *Celestial Navigation*, although it was hardest to write'; and critical opinion concurs that this is Tyler's best novel" (Mary Ellen Brooks, "Anne Tyler," in *The Dictionary of Literary Biography*, Vol. 6: *American Novelists Since World War II* [Detroit: Gale Research, 1980]: 342).

2. Brooks 344.

3. Brooks 341; and Wendy Lamb, "An Interview with Anne Tyler," *Iowa Journal of Literary Studies* 3 (1981): 64.

4. "When Tyler overcame her fear [of motherhood, of the possessions that accumulate when one has children, etc.], she immedi-

ately created her most genuinely lovable and contented mother, Mary, who innately needs six children and takes in boarders and waifs as well" (Margaret Morganroth Gullette, "The Tears (and Joys) Are in the Things: Adulthood in Anne Tyler's Novels," *New England Review and Bread Loaf Quarterly* 7 [Spring 1985]: 332).

5. Laurie L. Brown, "Interviews with Seven Contemporary Writers," *Southern Quarterly* 21 (Summer 1983): 4; Brooks 337.

6. Doris Betts, "The Fiction of Anne Tyler," *Southern Quarterly* 21 (Summer 1983): 30.

7. Quoted in Marguerite Michaels, "Anne Tyler, Writer 8:05 to 3:30," *New York Times Book Review* (8 May 1977): 43.

8. "I write sitting cross-legged on a very hard couch. I use a rectractable ball-point pen, for which I keep a constant store of two dozen refills (fine-tipped, black) in case the Parker Company suddenly goes out of business and leaves me helpless. These are the little rituals that make novelists look neurotic" (Anne Tyler, "Because I Want More Than One Life," *Washington Post* [15 August 1976], Sec. G: 1). These rituals may, however, change: "'I used to use Bics,' says Tyler, 'but after a few hours the ridges became painful'" (quoted in Michaels 42).

9. Tyler G1. By 1989, however, she had made one high-tech concession: she types up the holograph drafts of her novels on her word processor—"But even the rewrites have to be in longhand again" (Interview with AHP).

10. Michaels 42. The unusual hours reflect the fact that Tyler suffers from "an inherited family insomnia."

11. Tyler G7.

12. Michaels 43. For further discussions of Tyler's index card system, see Michaels 13, and Tyler G7. Anne Tyler also writes of her cards, and her abortive attempt to supplement them with a "midget tape recorder," in "Still Just Writing," in Janet Sternburg, ed., *The Writer on Her Work* (New York: Norton, 1980): 12, 9–10.

The orderliness of Tyler's work habits contrasts sharply with those of Jeremy. He has but one index card, tacked to the windowsill beside his bed, recording the truism ("Emerson's I think," says Tyler) that "a man could develop character by doing one thing he disliked every day of his life" (76, *87*). But Jeremy discovers, as Tyler explains, that "even getting out of bed is difficult, for him. He's already done something he disliked before his day is even begun" (quoted in Lamb 62). When Jeremy's sole card fell down behind his bed, "he let it lie" (100, *113*). The difference in their attitudes towards index cards is an important indication that, however superficially similar Tyler and Jeremy may be as creative individuals, she has more control and balance in both her personal life and her career.

As of August 1989, Tyler had this to say about her index card system: "I still use index cards, yes—but only in the most complicated chapters do I, or did I ever, bother numbering them" according to chapter and scene (Interview with AHP).

13. "I hate to travel away from here [her study]. I hate even to rearrange the furniture, or start writing at an unaccustomed time. All these magic spells [serve] to get me going" (Tyler, " 'Because I Want' " G1).

14. Quoted in Lamb 62–63.

15. Quoted in Brooks 341.

16. Tyler, "Still Just Writing" 13.

17. Quoted in Michaels 43.

18. Tyler, " 'Because I Want' " G1.

19. Tyler, "Still Just Writing" 7.

20. "I wish I weren't a writer every time the writing's over. The bad part comes when you have to deal with galley proofs, publicity, biographical sketches. I am protected (I am positively cushioned) by a very understanding agent, but still I'm forced to see what I've overlooked until now; these daydreams I've been weaving are no longer my private property" ("Because I Want" G7).

21. Compare, for example, Robert Frost's poem "Design" (1936). The speaker detects a pattern in the combination of the "dimpled spider, fat and white," the "white heal-all," and the moth "like a white piece of rigid satin cloth" (ll. 1–3), but he cannot determine the source behind the patterning. Perhaps, he surmises finally, it was "design of

darkness"—"If design govern in a thing so small" (ll. 13–14). That there may be no design at all underlying the deadly scene is arguably more frightening than the possibility that evil forces were responsible for it.

22. Jay L. Halio, "Love and the Grotesque," *Southern Review* 11 (Autumn 1975): 945.

23. Alan Pryce-Jones, "Five Easy Pieces: One Work of Art," *Washington Post Book World* (24 March 1974): 2.

24. Quoted in Lamb 61.

25. Tyler, "Still Just Writing" 9. Tyler's frank admission that having children had "slowed down" her career temporarily is quite different from Jeremy's terror that time spent with his family is time lost from his art. Even as he contemplated proposing to Mary, "he dreamed of losing things—unnamed objects in small boxes, the roof of his house, pieces of art that he would never be able to re-create" (91, *103*). He works frantically on his statue of the running man, fearing "that he might drop dead by nightfall, leaving his figure unfinished and his life in bits on the studio floor. . . . They would think the skeleton was what he had intended, with all its flaws. Surely, then, if ghosts existed he would have to become one; his restless spirit would be forced to return to haunt what he had left undone" (165, *184*). Tyler herself, writing not long after the publication of *Celestial Navigation*, admitted that she had come to the realization that she need no longer panic over being unable to get particular ideas down on paper: "It's begun to dawn on me that ideas are infinite in number, and more will always show up. I used to be afraid we had a limited lifetime supply" ("Because I Want" G1). Interestingly, she has since shifted her position on this matter. In 1981 Tyler reported that "I'm in a different state from the one I was in when I wrote all that [in 1976]. I'm more concerned about losing ideas" (quoted in Lamb 60).

26. Doris Betts argues that Jeremy's "development from collage to sculpture seems to parallel Tyler's literary progress from story to more and more complex novel," in particular in her tendency to increase "texture, depth, dimension, of the small, earthly possessions

which come to hand" (Betts 29, 31). Susannah Clapp makes a similar observation, arguing that *Celestial Navigation* "is made up, collage-like, of different though not incompatible views of life and Jeremy" ("In the Abstract," *[London] Times Literary Supplement* [23 May 1975]: 577).

CHAPTER SIX

Searching for Caleb

The contemporary critical response to Anne Tyler's sixth novel, *Searching for Caleb* (1976), was uniformly positive. Adjectives such as "charming," "old-fashioned," and "sunny" freckled the reviews, while John Updike, whose appraisals of Tyler's work in *The New Yorker* have done much to further her reputation and sales, lauded her seemingly encyclopedic knowledge of such Victoriana as the song "Just a Lock of Hair for Mother," folk remedies (amethyst glass, quassia cups), Belgian paving bricks, and horehound drops.[1] Tyler herself would seem to have confirmed the nostalgic cheeriness of *Searching for Caleb* by declaring it "the most fun" to write of all her novels, and by revealing that the prototype for Daniel Peck was her own beloved Grandfather Tyler who, unlike his fictional counterpart, had unfortunately lost most of his teeth.[2] So universally upbeat have been the commentaries on *Searching for Caleb* that it is difficult to read them without detecting almost a sigh of relief as Tyler, juggling the events of a full century in the lives of the Peck family of Baltimore, carefully avoids slashed foreheads, locust infestations, accidentally discharged pistols, and agoraphobic artists in the attic. To be sure, there is a suicide, that of the bereaved and beruffled Caroline Peck Mayhew; but otherwise the dark shadows on the sunny Peck world seem due to nothing more serious than Caleb's running away to New Orleans to play the blues, or Justine's socially dubious talent for telling fortunes, or Duncan's unfortunate fondness for bourbon. These are accessible problems, the critics would seem to be saying. These are not serious. These are "charming." Perhaps; but to so aver is to lose sight of the fact that *Searching for Caleb* tackles, more directly than ever before, serious concerns central to the Tyler canon: the complex relationships between the family and the individual self; the Hawthornesque burden of the past, coupled with a terror of the future; and the potential destructiveness inherent in such "good" things as loving one's children. Perhaps the best way to appreciate the mottled quality of this ostensibly sunny novel is to consider the Pecks as a family spanning five generations, as well as the two descendants who most clearly embody the best and worst that family has to offer: Justine and Duncan.

The founder of the Peck family line, Justin Montague Peck, carved his family's name and fortune out of the Baltimore business world of the 1870s much as Thomas Sutpen, of Faulkner's *Absalom, Absalom!* (1936), had carved his out of a Mississippi swamp. "Where he originally came from was uncertain" (53, *50*), but what was certain was that he made a fortune importing sugar, coffee, and guano—and that this was not sufficient to gain entry into Baltimore society, an entity "narrow and ossified even then" (53, *50*). So Justin Montague Peck created his own little microcosm of high society within his own family circle: he dedicated his life, and he expected his descendants to dedicate theirs, to polishing an aura of Peckish respectability and "good taste." Carefully selected outsiders were occasionally brought into the Peck inner circle. At age fifty, Justin chose as his bride the daughter of another importer, Sarah Cantleigh. Just sixteen years old, Sarah was pliant enough to enter fully into Justin's plan to establish a family dynasty, but rather too young for motherhood: she died in 1880 while giving birth to Daniel, just nine months after the wedding. Undaunted, Justin married within the year a somewhat older woman (age twenty), Laura Baum, of "stronger stock" (54, *51*). As the blunt biological terminology suggests, Justin regarded his marriages as matters of breeding, not love; and although he was correct in sensing the strength of Laura's German blood—she in fact would not die until 1958, aged nearly one hundred—he was incorrect in gauging the direction that strength would take. Knowing she could not challenge openly her intimidating husband, Laura became "mean and spiteful" (242, *234*) and refused, apparently, to submit to Justin's demands for reproduction. She had just one child, Caleb, born in 1885.

As is seen so often in literature depicting brothers (Jacob and Esau, Cain and Abel), the half-brothers Daniel and Caleb Peck have little in common, although, unlike most of these fraternal pairings, they are not rivals—a fact which would tend to counter any efforts to draw parallels between *Searching for Caleb* and John Steinbeck's *East of Eden* (1952), which traces the long-term rivalry between Aron and Caleb Trask. The lack of tension between the Peck sons seems due to the striking differences in their temperaments, differences which at first glance would seem to be attributable to their two mothers. Certainly Tyler appears to be downplaying the importance of environment, as both boys receive quality educations in Baltimore and are raised by Laura Baum Peck, who seems to love them equally. Justin Peck, however, responds to his sons quite differently. As a self-made man, Justin can appreciate and support his older son's desire to enter the law instead of importing, but he is far less flexible with his younger son: Daniel wanted to study law, "therefore Caleb would take over the importing business" (56, 53), whether he wanted to or not. In fact, he doesn't want to: he is temperamentally ill-suited to the world of commerce, but his father refuses to face this—especially in light of the fact that what he really wants is to pursue a career in music. This is attributed initially to his inheritance of "his Grandpa Baum's delight in noise and crowds. Even as a baby, being wheeled along in his caramel-colored wicker carriage, he would go into fits of glee at the sight of passing strangers. He liked anything musical—church bells, hurdy-gurdies, the chants of the street vendors selling hot crabcakes" (55, 52). Not the type to be holed up in a stuffy office all day, Caleb would absentmindedly wander off on his velocipede after any music he might hear, "speechless with joy, his appleseed eyes dancing" (55, 52). As his appleseed-brown eyes confirm, Caleb seems not to be what Tyler critics persist in terming a "true Peck."[3] Lacking the requisite Peck blue eyes and driving need for businesslike order, Caleb is exiled to the barn to play his cello, far from the ears of his father. Even a visit to the family's office fails to counter Caleb's love of music; and when he declares that he still wants to be a musician instead of an importer, his father suffers a paralytic stroke. "You have killed your half of your father," declares the distraught Laura (58, 55), but she is not quite accurate. In fact, Caleb has unwittingly resurrected and activated an aspect of Justin's temperament that he had been forced to repress years before.

For Caleb's love of music actually is not pure Baum; it is pure Peck. Though he had hidden it well, Justin Montague Peck seems himself to have been deeply enamored of music. When Caleb first began to learn ragtime from the family's Creole gardener, Lafleur Boudrault, Justin had simply "shrugged it off" (57, 53).

This is not the response of a business-minded music-hater, but its implications become clear only after his stroke. Daniel's wife Margaret Rose installs a Graphophone in Justin's sickroom, and "it amused the old man for hours on end. He seemed particularly fond of Caruso. He would order Margaret to stand beside his bed cranking the machine and changing the heavy black discs. Margaret was surprised. If this was the way he felt, why had he forbidden Caleb's music in the house?" (62, 59). The answer is that the "uncertain" background of Justin Peck evidently included a passion for music, one that simply could not co-exist peacefully with his equally strong passion for business. Essentially a dichotomous man,[4] Justin realized that to succeed as an importer required the deliberate repression of his musicality. Only when the stroke made it impossible for him to get to the office did Justin acknowledge once again his love for music. But the business side of him, the side inherited primarily by Daniel, had not been silenced. Unwilling to face the fact that Caleb had inherited primarily his musical side, and refusing to surrender his dream of a Peck dynasty founded on importing, Justin is furious that Caleb will not sacrifice music for business as he himself had done. Even when Caleb begins going to his father's office in dutiful guilt after Justin's collapse, the old man still rejects him, staring at the bedroom wall when his brown-eyed son visits him.

Caleb, meanwhile, does not comprehend that his father's coolness towards him reflects the old man's own sense of personal loss. He continues to go to his roll-top desk in Justin's office, "already tired and beaten-looking" (65, 62) when he leaves for work in the morning, and returning home in various stages of inebriation. The one bright spot in his life is his sister-in-law Margaret Rose, another imported breeder who dutifully produces six little Pecks, including eldest son "Justin Two" and the family's perennial baby, Caroline. "Things were working out just fine," in the opinion of Justin Peck. "Everything was going according to plan" (61, 58), including the construction of a cluster of magnificent homes in the wilds of Roland Park. But eventually Margaret Rose abandons her family to return to her mother in Washington, the first of a series of Peck runaways. She dies in a fire in 1912, the same year that Caleb disappears without a trace. But the Peck dynasty marches on, in the form of Daniel and those children who seem to embody the rigid, orderly business half of Justin Montague Peck just as surely as Caleb embodies the intuitive musical half.

Having spent his childhood safely at home perusing that ultra-conservative juvenile periodical *The Youth's Companion*, Daniel went on to join a respectable law firm and to marry a woman chosen for him by his father ("Justin planned to have a great many descendants and he was anxious to get them started" [60, 57]). Appropriately, Daniel becomes a judge, an occupation well-suited to his temperamental inclination to pass judgments on everything from buses ("An inferior class of people tended to travel by bus" [155, *149*]) to visitors ("People who were not related to him ought to keep to themselves, he always said" [23, *21*]). This same judgmental nature is evident in his children, who by upbringing and inherited temperament have fixed notions about virtually everything:

"[W]e've all been taught that we disapprove of sports cars, golf, women in slacks, chewing gum, the color chartreuse, emotional displays, ranch houses, bridge, mascara, household pets, religious discussions, plastic, politics, nail polish, transparent gems of any color, jewelry shaped like animals, checkered prints . . . we're all told from birth on that no Peck has had a cavity in all recorded history or lost a single tooth; that we're unfailingly punctual even when we're supposed to come late; that we write our bread-and-butter notes no more than an hour after every visit; that we always say 'Baltimore' instead of 'Balmer'; that even when we're wearing our ragged old gardening clothes you can peek down our collars and see 'Brooks Brothers' on the label, and our boots are English and meant for riding though none of us has ever sat on a horse . . ." (93, *88–89*, ellipses in the original)

Daniel and his descendants drive only Fords, wash only with Ivory soap, write only on cream-colored stationery, and cook only with Fannie Farmer recipes. They never throw away wrapping paper; they never use public facilities; and they never put religious art in the living room "unless it [is] an original" (229, 221). The farcical nature of this litany of *do*'s and *don't*'s should not obscure the fact that most of these regulations had meaningful, practical origins. For example, when Ivory soap entered the market at the turn of the century, it was heralded for its purity ("so pure, it floats") at a time when there were no government regulations regarding additives. But these preferences have fanned out beyond practicality and quality to include such silly matters as animal-shaped jewelry and plaids. Worse, these preferences have hardened into virtual laws.

Did the matter stop at soap brands and colors, the Pecks might indeed seem like a charmingly eccentric clan, but unfortunately it extends even to attitudes and perception. This is particularly evident in their terror of three interrelated matters: outsiders, change, and travel. Once again, the origins of these fears were quite practical. Justin Montague Peck had good reason to steer clear of outsiders. Involved in a business known for keen competitiveness, he chose to stay home entirely after his stroke because "he could not bear to have his weakness observed by the outside world (which would take advantage immediately, he was certain of it)" (58, 55). His tendency to turn inward, to establish a closed family unit in which he could function safely, was thus a matter of business necessity as much as a response to the closure of Baltimore high society. Further, Justin was not personally averse to travel: he enjoyed his daily trips to the Merchants' Exchange, and he seems to have been drawn to importing precisely because of the vicarious travel involved. The Peck ships, those "fullrigged steamers" which "looked like brigantines with smokestacks," made "spectacular journeys to Brazil and Peru and the West Indies." Though the operation eventually was cut back to "the more profitable coastwise hauls" (57, *53–54*), the fact remains that Justin dealt every day with people and with change in a business noted for the most exciting voyages of the era.

His descendants seem to have lost his receptivity to travel and change while gripping ever more tightly to his understandable mistrust of outsiders. This is conveyed in the behavior of his grandson, Justin Two. Simply called "Two," he ventures from the family compound in Roland Park just once a year, to visit his father Daniel on his birthday. As is signified by the dropping of his Christian name, Two has little in common with his energetic forebear and namesake: he drives at a "stately tempo" (204, *196*)—read "dangerously slow"—in his Ford, a car make chosen simply because all Pecks own Fords. His wife Lucy, yet another outsider imported precisely because of her bland receptivity to Peckish ways, dreads the prospect of a day of travel amongst unknown outsiders, and yearns to be back at the family compound in Roland Park:

Lucy longed for her wing chair in which she could sit encircled, almost, with the wings working like a mule's

blinders to confine her gaze to the latest historical romance. . . . And it was so much cooler and greener at
home, so shadowy, so thickly treed that when you
spoke outdoors your voice came echoing back, clear and
close . . . (204, *196–97*)

A location that offers security to the point of agoraphobic isolation and narcissism (hence the echoes), the
house features even the kind of chair that has
"blinders"—perfect for a family that has reduced Justin
Montague Peck's "sharp-eyed" perceptiveness (53, *50*)
into a kind of tunnel vision.

That tunnel vision extends not just to car makes
and colors, but more dramatically to time. The Pecks
on Daniel's side of the family are past-oriented, a situation that would have horrified a man like Justin Montague Peck who lived in the day-to-day immediacy of
the business world while working towards a secure future for his descendants. Instead, they look back to him,
what with their historical romances and appropriately
faded-looking cream-colored stationery. Their oak-lined
homes are the homes he ordered built in once-secluded
Roland Park after the Great Fire of 1904. Their permanently dusty furniture is the furniture he bought;
indeed, everything in their side-by-side houses is offi-
cially antique, as young Duncan is well aware: "no one
bought anything; the rooms were crowded with mel-
lowed, well-kept furniture that appeared to have grown
there, and whenever children departed they took sev-

eral pieces with them but left the rooms as crowded as ever, somehow, as if more had sprouted in the night" (36, 33). Even the jewelry that his aunts wear "every day of their lives," like Victorian slide pendants, is literally antique (190, 183). So desperately is Daniel's clan oriented towards the past, so infantilizing is their habit of avoiding people and change in the outside world, that they seem to resist growing old. Whereas commonplace outsiders are subject to what the Pecks regard as "premature aging" (37, 34), they themselves seem to live forever in their dusty world, their "blue, blue eyes" (26, 24) always young and their occasional wrinkles ceasing at the optimum tasteful moment. Daniel's wrinkles, for example, "had reached a saturation point"; no new ones "had been added in years." In fact, he looks the same age as his son, Two: "In the end, the quarter-century that divided their generations amounted to nothing and was swept away" (208–09, 201).

Co-existing with their orientation towards the past is their obsession with the present—or, more precisely, with the exact present moment, as an entity in itself. Daniel and his clan pride themselves on owning accurate timepieces and being always punctual. Once again, these were desirable qualities for a businessman like Justin Montague Peck, but his descendants have refined them to an obsessive level. Daniel sports a snaptop pocket watch, thanks to which he is able to report the exact moment: "Ah! Five twelve" (188, 181). However, in his focus on the precise moment, Daniel does not

realize what is going on during it: the unwanted elopement of his great-granddaughter Meg. Nor does he perceive the bigger picture of time passing. Once Caleb is
located in 1973, for example, Daniel is stunned to realize
that his brother would now be eighty-eight years old.
Even Caleb, gone for sixty-one years, still pictures his
childhood home the way it was, "a house with cloth
dolls and hobbyhorses scattered across the lawn" (288,
279). Significantly, Daniel cannot handle this jolt of reality, this confirmation of time passing. He fears the
longed-for reunion with Caleb, arguing that "it would
be so tiring, having to bring him up to date on all that's
happened. Too much has gone on. I might not know
him. He might not know *me*. I might look old to him"
(257–58, *249*). Rather than face his brother and the passage of time that he represents, Daniel suddenly dies.
In contrast, the more free-spirited Caleb refuses to
dwell on the past. "He preferred the present" (278, *268*),
and actively welcomed the change embodied in the future. This double preference is strong enough to enable
him to escape from the rest home in Box Hill with
Justine, to decline being reunited with his past-obsessed
family in Roland Park, and to move to Wyoming to start
a new life, though he is almost ninety years old. These
dichotomies—the Danielesque inertia versus the
Calebesque restlessness, the Danielesque past/present
orientation versus the Calebesque present/future one—
constitute the Peck totality. But they are extremely difficult to integrate, as Justin Montague Peck knew well.

SEARCHING FOR CALEB

Both the Peck dichotomies and the impulse to integrate them into a meaningful whole are evident in the novel's two protagonists, Justine and Duncan.

Although born a Mayhew in 1933 and raised in Philadelphia, Justine seemed in her childhood and young womanhood to be the embodiment of all that her grandfather Daniel Peck represents. She adores horehound drops, coffee beans, root beer, and Luden's cough drops, a preference shared by her grandfather ("he liked herby things" [7, 5]). She learns of life not through interactions with outsiders, but through magazines: *Mademoiselle* when she is a young miss, *Bride's* when she is engaged, and *Woman's Day* when she is first married. (Once she begins her search for Caleb with Daniel, she switches to *National Geographic*.) She dutifully dislikes diamonds, one of those dreaded transparent gemstones. She always wears a Breton hat, "perfectly level" (92, *87*), because all Peck women wear hats. She drives a Ford. She wears only those clothes selected for her by her mother, Caroline Peck Mayhew. And she dazzles her first sweetheart, Neely Carpenter, by Peckishly announcing one day after church that "It's approximately twelve thirteen and a half" (83, *79*). Justine seems, indeed, to be well on her way to following in the footsteps of her drab, silent, spinster Peck aunts, Laura May and Sarah.

But beneath her placid Peckish exterior is another Justine, one that is ill at ease with life in the Danielesque mode. The "bearded men" (67, *64*) whom she fears hide under her bed reflect her acute distress. Granted, part of her distress stems from her uncertain relationship with her mother, the Peck family baby. But Justine's uncertainty regarding her mother's love, her frantic search for the "magic password" (70, 66) that would make all well in their relationship, is only one source of her troubled state. What is more important is that, unknown even to her, she harbors impulses that would render her as much akin to Caleb as to Daniel. These impulses are activated by her first cousin, Duncan Peck.

From the outset, Duncan was nothing like the Danielesque Pecks; in fact, he was actively antagonistic towards them. "A Peck's bad boy,"[5] he made Grandfather Daniel a Noxzema and olive sandwich for a family picnic. Unlike his reclusive relatives, he was constantly bringing home such unsavory outsiders as "ten-year-old boys with tobacco breath and BB guns and very poor grammar" (77, 73). When older, he announced his decision to study science instead of entering the law (it had become the "new" Peck tradition when the importing business was sold), and he spitefully drove around in "a forty-dollar 1933 Graham Paige that smelled suspiciously of beer" (81, 77) simply because it was not a Ford: "I have a deep-seated *hatred* of Fords" (166, 159). What he really hates, of course, is the most neurotic and inflexible aspects of the Danielesque side of the Peck family, their tunnel vision, past orientation, and terror of outsiders and of change. So when the first opportunity arises, Duncan runs away, to live in a tiny apartment near Johns Hopkins. Justine visits him there, at first because her family tells her to and because her Danielesque side longs to see order restored, but then because he opens her eyes to other possibilities, to the side of her Peck nature that made Caleb a happy wandering minstrel. Under Duncan's influence, Justine begins "watching her aunts and uncles in a measuring way that made them uncomfortable" (97, 92). She begins being tardy for classes at her junior college: "Is that what you call the point of life?," Justine demands suddenly. "Getting to a class on the dot of nine o'clock?" (100, 95–96). And perhaps most dramatic of all, she has sex with Duncan, feeling "happy and certain" despite her inexperience, "a naked girl wearing a Breton hat" (102, 98).

But as the trademark hat suggests, Justine's recognition of her free-spirited Calebesque side does not mean an automatic, total rejection of the more conservative Danielesque one. She insists upon marrying Duncan in a church, wearing Sarah Cantleigh Peck's veil. She accepts the customary donation of antique Peck furniture, none of which is appropriate for the tiny three-bedroom cabin on her new goat farm. She dutifully tries to learn to cook using the Pecks' preferred Fannie Farmer cookbook. She continues to drive Ford cars. And she feels the customary Peck guilt when her father dies suddenly of a heart attack and her bereaved mother kills herself: "[Caroline] had to wait for six cars, all told, before she found one that would run her down" (124, *118*).

Even so, the long-repressed Calebesque free-spirit-edness begins to assert itself. Once their marriage gets under way, neither Justine nor Duncan wears a watch. Justine acquiesces happily when Duncan decides to grow sweet corn on the front lawn. She is delighted to move from town to town, job to job, as Duncan indulges his characteristic restlessness. Rejecting Fannie Farmer, Justine eventually ceases cooking altogether: most of her nourishment comes from Luden's cough drops and Cheez Doodles. And most important of all, she takes up fortune telling, an activity which, like Caleb's music, requires both skill and intuition. No longer burdened by the past—indeed, every time they moved, "they left more and more things behind" (153, *146*)—and no longer intimidated by the future, she advises her clients to "Take the change. Always change" (32, *29*).

But just as there are dangers accompanying the Danielesque tendency towards inertia and isolation, there are problems inherent in the Calebesque side of the Peck temperament. Those dangers are especially obvious in Duncan. An "aging little boy" (221, *213*), Duncan is incapable of following through with an intelligent plan of action. Always chasing rainbows, he embarks on a series of careers selected precisely because he knows nothing about them. Bewitched by the idea of raising chickens, for example, "Duncan bought a dozen copper-colored hens and installed them in a shed he had built himself, complete with a box of oyster shells to assist in egg production and a zinc watering trough in which they all immediately drowned" (129, *123*). If, by some fluke, a career begins to be successful, he drops it to pursue another. He abandons his goat farm, for example, when there is sudden local interest in his cheeses and goat milk. And he quits the Blue Bottle antique shop when it begins to thrive: "Once the shop had proved a success, [its owner] *expected* things of Duncan. He was always waiting to hear good news. Duncan couldn't stand to have things expected of him. . . . He felt the air turning gluey with the weight of other people's disapproval, suspicions, hopes, preconceived notions" (270, *261*). The same impulse towards evasion is evident in other areas. Duncan is a compulsive liar, and rather than discuss anything substantive he engages others in pointless arguments, claiming that English spelling is illogical ("'a waste of letters'" [142, *137*]) and that Christianity is "a dying religion" (114, *109*)—something appreciated by the Rev. Didicott almost as much as the fifty dollars in Confederate money that Duncan paid him for the wedding. Constantly on the run and incapable of dealing with either the past or the future, Duncan sinks more and more deeply into endless games of solitaire, bottles of bourbon, and marijuana.

Justine's father, Sam Mayhew, had spoken more

rightly than he knew when he warned her that Duncan wanted to marry her for "one of two reasons. Either he wants a Peck along to torment, or to lean on. Either he's going to give you hell or else he's knotted tighter to his family than he thinks he is" (113, *108*). The knot truly is at issue, for Duncan is more like Daniel Peck than this compulsive liar cares to admit. Indeed, even his quasi-incestuous marriage to his first cousin is typically Danielesque: "this way there's no adjustment for [Justine and Duncan] to make, no in-law problems" (104, *99*)—in other words, no outside reality to contend with. This is seen further in the fact that Duncan takes jobs only with relatives. Silas Amsel, owner of the Blue Bottle, is his "mother's sister's brother-in law": " 'We've used up all my mother's *blood* relations,' Duncan said cheerfully" (29, *27*). Further, his constant movement is, as Frank W. Shelton points out, "a way of separating himself from others."[6] Even the corn he grows in his front yard is every bit as isolationist as his mother's wing chair: "their corn was so tall it blocked their view of the street. Cars swished by unseen, almost un-heard. . . . People walking past were no more than dis-embodied voices" (224, *217*). And, as Mary Ellen Brooks observes, in opposing his daughter Meg's marriage to Rev. Arthur Milsom, Duncan is "saying essentially the same things Justine's father had said to her about her choice for a husband. Duncan's negative response to Meg and her fiance reveals that he [is] as narrow-minded as the Pecks he ran away from."[7]

SEARCHING FOR CALEB

What is worse, as Duncan becomes increasingly drawn to close-minded Danielesque conservatism under the self-deluding guise of Calebesque free-spiritedness, Justine is dragged along with him. Entering fully into his compulsion to keep moving, the once-serene Justine "gave an impression of energy burning and wasting. She moved very fast and accomplished very little" (19, *17–18*). In the process, she barely connects with her daughter Meg, that Danielesque child who asked for a toaster for her seventh birthday and dutifully shampoos her hair every Monday and Thursday. During Meg's greatest crisis, her showdown with her father over her engagement to Arthur Milsom, Justine was not present. Even when Meg located her immediately thereafter, in the kitchen learning I Ching using raw spaghetti, Justine was unable to understand or respond to the severity of the situation:

"I just want to tell you this," Meg said. "I blame you as much as him."

"What, Meggie dear?"

"The two of you are as closed as a unit can get, I don't care *what* he says."

"Closed? What?" said Justine, looking bewildered. (179, *172*)

After Meg's elopement, Justine recalls a revealing visit to a New Jersey lighthouse. In her determination to race to the top, Justine had completely forgotten about little

Meg, left sobbing on the next to the last flight of stairs: "But had that taught [Justine] anything? She had only speeded up with every year, gathering momentum. Racing toward some undefined future and letting the past roll up behind her, swooping Meg along under one arm but neglecting to listen to her or to ask if she wanted this trip at all." As a result, "Meg grew up alone, self-reared, and left home alone for a sad stunted life she had not really wanted," while Grandfather Daniel accompanied Justine and Duncan on their endless moves. Finally, "Justine awoke one day to wonder how it had happened: what she had mislaid was Justine herself" (266, *258*).

To be Calebesque is thus to run the risk of being irresponsible, selfish, flighty. Justine comes to recognize the emergence of these qualities in herself, and it leaves her first distracted, unable to read fortunes with her usual care and gusto, and then upset. Indeed, although she originally had been delighted to rescue Caleb from his Louisiana rest home, once their contact increases she experiences a dramatic change of heart:

She had to admit there were times when Caleb disappointed her.
No, more than that. Tell the truth. There were times when she almost disliked him. (300, *290*)

After all, Caleb had proven himself to be "adaptable, endlessly adaptable":

SEARCHING FOR CALEB

As Justine herself had.

Then a trembling would rise from the soles of her feet, turn her stomach queasy, pass through the hollow of her chest to beat in her throat like a second heart. (301, *291*)

In nurturing the most irresponsible aspects of her Calebesque side, she had lost the most stabilizing aspects of the Danielesque, just as surely as her ancestor and namesake, Justin Montague Peck, had actively repressed the creative and intuitive half of his temperament in favor of the more conservative business-oriented half. Justine will try to do what Justin could not: to select out the most desirable qualities of each half, to nurture them, and to re-integrate them into a healthy whole. In short, she must relocate the "mislaid" Peck self.

In "searching for Caleb" in the company of an ancestor, Grandfather Daniel Peck, Justine is searching for that mislaid self. Surely it is no accident that the title of Tyler's novel echoes *Waiting for Godot*, Samuel Beckett's famed play, for many of the issues Tyler raises are indeed existential in nature. As Catherine Peters points out in the [*London*] *Times Literary Supplement*,

It becomes clear in the course of this robust, witty novel that Anne Tyler is concerned with an existential examination of the nature of freedom. The choices, between staying put and running away, conforming or rebelling, are not as simple as they seem, perhaps not in themselves important: it is the use made of them that matters.[8]

Tyler herself seems quite conscious of this aspect of her novel, as she has Justine, steadily leaving behind more Peck impedimenta and abandoning repetitive routines like cooking, wonder "if just *being* were enough to take all her time and attention" (153, *147*). Determining the answer and then translating it into meaningful, purposeful action is the central issue of the book, and it seems particularly compounded as Justine witnesses Duncan's Danielesque and Calebesque undesirable qualities becoming mutually destructive. But ultimately Justine finds the answer: they will join Alonzo's carnival, with Duncan putting to good use his genuine knack for things mechanical, and Justine putting to good use her own sound judgment and intuition as a fortune teller. Life in a "forty-miler" carnival with an established home base in Maryland is the ideal symbol of integration, offering them "both permanence and change, identity and variety, home and lots of travel."[9]

The ending of the novel is not, as Martha B. Tack would have it, "wonderfully inconclusive."[10] Justine has focused upon the one mode of living that would enable her and Duncan to rein in the worst aspects of Danielesque and Calebesque Peckness while nurturing the best. They are not denying their Peck identities: like Caleb's farewell bread-and-butter note, some of the family's tastes and habits will never leave her. But as Madame Olita suggested years earlier, Justine can *select* which ones will stay: she cannot change the past, the Peck tradition, but she can change "what hold it has on you" (135, *129*).

Of course, the other Pecks seem unable to achieve this integrative, emotionally healthy vision. While Caleb remains insistently Calebesque, the others (including Meg) remain Danielesque. The sterility of their one-sidedness is reflected in the family tree. Shaped like a diamond, a jewel the Pecks have been taught to despise, the family tree embroidered by Aunt Laura May symbolically leaves no room for any children to be born to Meg and Arthur. Like the Pyncheons in *The House of the Seven Gables*, the once-powerful Pecks will fade into an oblivion as complete as that out of which Justin Montague Peck emerged a century before. Tyler seems not to find this tragic. A family dynasty, however wealthy or imbued with "good taste," is not necessarily conducive to the nurturance of the individual self. And the dynamics of that nurturance is a central element of Anne Tyler's fictional vision.

Notes

1. Barbara A. Bannon, for example, sees the characters as "charming eccentrics" ([rev. of *Searching for Caleb*], *Publishers Weekly*

208 [3 November 1975]: 63). Lynn Sharon Schwartz remarks that the novel offers "the very welcome old-fashioned virtues of a patient, thoughtful chronicle" ([rev. of *Searching for Caleb*], *Saturday Review* 3 [6 March 1976]: 28). Katha Pollitt terms it "Tyler's sunniest, most expansive book" ([rev. of *Searching for Caleb*], *New York Times Book Review* [18 January 1976]: 22). John Updike, "Family Ways," *The New Yorker* 52 (29 March 1976): 110–12.

2. Quoted in Wendy Lamb, "An Interview with Anne Tyler," *Iowa Journal of Literary Studies* 3 (1981): 64; and in Mary Ellen Brooks, "Anne Tyler," in *The Dictionary of Literary Biography*, Vol. 6: *American Novelists Since World War II* (Detroit: Gale Research, 1980): 342. The prototype for Caleb was Tyler's great-grandfather, whose sepia photograph, showing him playing the cello in the hayloft door of a barn, hangs in her Baltimore study (Marguerite Michaels, "Anne Tyler, Writer 8:05 to 3:30," *New York Times Book Review* [8 May 1977]: 42).

3. Both Brooks (343) and Pollitt (22) use the term to mean what is identified throughout this chapter as "Danielesque" qualities of the Peck temperament, as opposed to "Calebesque" ones. A "true Peck" actually would combine both.

4. Stella Nesanovich recognizes that "while the Peck family appears homogeneous in character, in point of fact it is dichotomous, with [Caleb] representing the nomadic, free-spirited, and musical side of the family." Nesanovich is mistaken, however, in maintaining that Duncan and Justine "have inherited some of Caleb's waywardness," for in fact they inherited both sides of Peckness. The novel shows them struggling to function while embodying the antithetical sides of the Peck temperament. (See "The Individual in the Family: Anne Tyler's *Searching for Caleb* and *Earthly Possessions*," *Southern Review* 14 [January 1978]: 171.)

5. Victor Howes, "Freedom: Theme of Pecks' Battle Hymns," *Christian Science Monitor* 68 (14 January 1976): 23. It is entirely possible that the "Peck's bad boy" joke was intentional. Tyler is, after all, the woman who wrote a novel about self-reliance featuring the Emerson family.

6. Frank W. Shelton, "The Necessary Balance: Distance and Sympathy in the Novels of Anne Tyler," *Southern Review* 20 (Autumn 1984): 857.

7. Brooks 343.

8. Catherine Peters, "Opting Out," *[London] Times Literary Supplement* (27 August 1976): 1060.

9. Anne G. Jones, "Home at Last, and Homesick Again: The Ten Novels of Anne Tyler," *The Hollins Critic* 23 (April 1986): 7.

10. Martha B. Tack, "Pecking Order," *The Village Voice* 21 (1 November 1976): 95.

CHAPTER SEVEN

Earthly Possessions and *Morgan's Passing*

What was identified as an existential dimension to *Searching for Caleb*—broadly speaking, a concern with the nature of both freedom and "being"—is even more pronounced in Anne Tyler's next two novels, *Earthly Possessions* (1977) and *Morgan's Passing* (1980). It is, in fact, perhaps too pronounced: both technically and thematically, they are self-conscious performances which rely too heavily on the use of a hostage situation to probe the nature of freedom and on the use of costumes to probe the nature of being. Even Tyler's most ardent supporters seemed taken aback by these novels, desperately maintaining that even she was entitled to an occasional lapse or, less charitably, that she had somehow lost control over her own material.[1] To be sure, the years surrounding their composition were unsettled ones: *Morgan's Passing* was continually interrupted by domestic crises which undermined Tyler's work schedule, a serious problem for a writer who relies heavily on a regular routine.[2] Further, during the three years between the two books' publications Tyler had in fact

EARTHLY POSSESSIONS AND *MORGAN'S PASSING*

written another novel, *Pantaleo,* one so poor that she voluntarily declined to publish it. Even more than a false start, a "ditched" novel can seriously undermine a writer's confidence and equanimity, and it is to her credit that Tyler was able to rally her energies to create *Morgan's Passing* after investing an entire year of her life in a failed project.[3] But the strain of the interim after *Searching for Caleb* is nonetheless evident: *Earthly Possessions* is physically and thematically a slight book, more novella than novel, and so transparent in its meaning that it verges on allegory.[4] *Morgan's Passing* is little better: "unruly and untidy," it is over-long, repetitious, and, at times, wearying to read.[5] Even so, *Earthly Possessions* and *Morgan's Passing* are not, as some critics would have it, either pointless or static. Neither is *Earthly Possessions* just another "runaway housewife" novel, any more than *Morgan's Passing* is just another account of a man suffering from the "middle-age crazies."[6] Rather, each offers a serious account of characters grappling with difficult problems involving the challenges of accommodating the needs of the self to the needs of the family and community, and of discovering the nature of personal freedom. At the same time, these characters face the necessity of determining, in both of these arenas, the difference between passivity and endurance, that point at which tolerance for life's inevitable disorder and change blurs from virtue to vice. Though neither *Earthly Possessions* nor *Morgan's Passing* is of the first rank in the Tyler canon, they do have value in their capacity to clarify and articulate ideas towards which she had been working since her first novel was published in 1964. In turn, these ideas would be important components of what are generally regarded as Tyler's three most mature efforts: *Dinner at the Homesick Restaurant, The Accidental Tourist,* and the Pulitzer Prize winning *Breathing Lessons.*

At first glance, *Earthly Possessions* would seem to be a dramatic departure for Anne Tyler. Whereas her earlier novels were built around such families as the Hawkeses, the Pikes, the Emersons, and the Pecks, *Earthly Possessions* concentrates intensively on the relationship between just two characters, Charlotte Ames Emory and Jake Simms, the bank robber who has taken her hostage. But closer inspection reveals that the novel is very much in the Tyler mode: a similar double protagonist format had been used to good effect in *A Slipping-Down Life,* while *Earthly Possessions* ranges beyond that earlier effort to explore not just the rise of a sense of self, but its rise within the context of family and community—two entities whose needs and demands often are at cross-purposes to those of the self. With her inherited house, library job, and neither bungling parents nor unfaithful husband to complicate matters for her, Evie Decker has been left free to nurture her selfhood within a materially secure and emotionally stable vacuum. But the actual world is of course more complicated, and Tyler explores those complications in *Earthly Possessions,* a book whose title betokens the material and emotional impedimenta of quotidian reality. It is thus a more fundamentally truthful book, although Charlotte herself has great difficulty establishing what the truth actually is.

Much of Charlotte's problem stems from her family situation. Born to a chronically depressed portrait photographer and "a fat lady who used to teach first grade"—"Notice that I mention her fatness first. You couldn't overlook fatness like my mother's" (11, *9*)—Charlotte grows up convinced that she is not their "true" daughter. Though her father tries to convince her otherwise by showing Charlotte her baby clothes, hardly proof positive of the wearer's identity, her mother is convinced (as was Mrs. Emerson) that there had been a mix-up at the hospital—or, more precisely, Charlotte *believes* that her mother is convinced of this. It will take the entire book for Charlotte to accept the realization that her perception of her identities as the "false" daughter of the Ameses and the helpless wife of Rev. Saul Emory has been distortive for years—and that she is largely responsible for it.

Hence the importance of Tyler's narrative structure. *Earthly Possessions* is told in the first-person, with chapters alternating between present action (Charlotte's kidnapping by Jake) and flashback (her recollections of her childhood, adolescence, and marriage). Her memories are as vivid as her perception of her kidnapping; unfortunately they also are incorrect, and it requires the physical distance of the journey from Maryland to Florida, the stress of knowing that she could be killed at any moment, and the dramatic shifts in point of view—seeing tapes of herself and Jake on the evening news, watching a televised interview with Saul, observing Jake's fearful submission to marriage with the pregnant Mindy—to jolt Charlotte into facing both that she has a strong "true" self beyond her seeming alienation and passivity, and that the Ameses and Saul have been damaging to her sense of selfhood only because she perceives them as such. Even blunt revelations of the truth by those around her prior to the kidnapping had failed to correct her blurred perception. Charlotte's brother-in-law Amos, visiting her home in Maryland and hence technically an outsider, points out that it is ludicrous for her to consider herself to be just filling in for her father in his photographic studio. After all, it is how she has been earning her living for years, and her father is long dead:

"This studio's been yours for, what? Sixteen, seventeen years now. It's been yours nearly as long as it was his."

"Well," I said. "Yes, but . . ." I turned and looked at him. "That's true, it has," I said.

"And still you act surprised when somebody wants you to take his picture. You have to decide if you'll do it, every time. A seventeen-year temporary position! Lord God." (204–05, *184*)

EARTHLY POSSESSIONS AND *MORGAN'S PASSING*

Even more dramatically, Charlotte should have begun to perceive herself as her parents' biological child when she learned that the old photograph she located, presumably that of the Ameses' "true" daughter, is actually a picture of her own mother. Mrs. Ames in fact bluntly denies that she had ever thought there was a mix-up at the hospital. But since this admission came when she was disoriented from cancer, and since old perceptions do die hard, Charlotte is unable to accept the full impact of the revelation. Unable, that is, until the kidnapping—and the input from Jake Simms.

As so often happens in Tyler's writings (and, indeed, in Flannery O'Connor's), epiphanies come from unlikely sources; or as John Updike phrases the matter, occasionally "bursts of articulate insight . . . overtake even the dim-witted" in her novels.[7] Jake has not fared well at the hands of critics, one of whom dismisses him as a "crazy dishonest boob";[8] but this is unfair and inaccurate, for Jake is much like Charlotte, right down to their "identical white shirts" (107, *96*). They both are driving in the demolition derby of life, with the important difference that Jake can explain to her the implications of what she is observing. She, for example, responds negatively to Saul's televised interview, interpreting literally his remark that she is a "good woman." But Jake recognizes that Saul is using goodness abstractly—in fact, much as Charlotte herself does when she asserts that she can be a "good woman" even if she is too much a non-believer to enter heartily into his world as pastor of the Holy Basis Church. "I've come to stand for everything bad," Charlotte explains to Jake. "I think [Saul] sees me as evil":

> "But then how come he said all that on TV?" Jake asked.
> I had trouble breaking off my train of thought. I said, "What?"
> "Said you was a good woman."
> "Oh . . . did he? I don't know, I guess he just meant I wouldn't have robbed a bank."
> "Then why didn't he *say* you wouldn't have robbed a bank?" said Jake. "What his words were, you're a good woman."
> I looked at him.
> "Maybe he sees things different now you've left," said Jake. "Or more likely, you just had him figured wrong to start with. I mean, it could be he really does believe you're good, and worries what that means for *his* side. Ever thought of that?"
> "Well, no." I said. (182–83, *163–64*)

On the strength of Jake's revelation, Charlotte's perception of her world suddenly shifts. She comes to feel that she might have had a happy childhood after all; she begins to appreciate the loving sacrifices made on her behalf by her mother ("I had never put it all together before" [194, *173*]); and she even qualifies the blunt fact with which she had begun the flashback sequences about her childhood: "Maybe I'd made up [my

EARTHLY POSSESSIONS AND *MORGAN'S PASSING*

mother's] fatness, too" (202, *182*). True, these things had begun to dawn on her before the kidnapping, but they had resulted only in disorientation and fear. She suddenly wanted to strip her house of all its belongings ("What I was aiming for was a house with the bare, polished look of a bleached skull" [206–07, *186*]) and to run away, an impulse seemingly confirmed by the discovery in her cereal box of a "Keep on Truckin'" badge. But only under the stress of the kidnapping does Charlotte come to realize that facing the truth need not, and indeed cannot, justify denying one's "earthly possessions" and frantically running away. Readjustment is part of the natural order of human life, and Charlotte returns home with a clearer vision of her childhood, of her relationship with Saul, and of the place of her own self within these contexts. Her two distinct "voices" in this novel—one "wry, humorous, distanced, self-deprecating," the other "richer, more various, and more deeply felt"—betoken this new perception, as Charlotte changes from a "passive and unreliable narrator" into an "active and reliable" one.[9]

It takes Morgan Gower one hundred pages more than Charlotte Emory to establish his true self and to reconcile it with the demands of family and community, but then his situation is more problematic. Whereas Charlotte's response to her difficulties had been passivity and despair followed by the compulsion to strip her home and run, Morgan's response is to remain in a physically limited area (roughly the environs of his Colonial home and hardware store) while assuming a series of different disguises. His "escape" is thus more mental than physical. Rising in the morning, he "decid[es] who to be today" by perusing his closet packed with "sailor outfits, soldier outfits, riverboat-gambler outfits" and hats "stacked six deep on the self" (29, *27–28*). Were it simply a matter of deciding whether to wear his gnome hat, sombrero, or Panama, Morgan might indeed be a lovable eccentric of the sort rarely seen in contemporary American fiction.[10] However, he goes beyond mere costumes to assumed identities—and he does it so convincingly that several reviewers take literally his identification of himself as "Gower Morgan" (21, *19*).[11] It is while posing as Gower Morgan, M.D., that he delivers Emily Cathcart Meredith's daughter Gina in the opening chapter of the novel—a situation which, though it turned out fine, is potentially dangerous to both mother and baby. Childbirth is emphatically real; and in maintaining incorrectly that the baby could not possibly be born before their arrival at the hospital, Morgan Gower shows himself unable to deal with reality: denial, as emblematized by his costumes and his assumed personae (French artist, priest, rabbi, cobbler, mailman), is his preferred mode of not facing his lack of control over his world and his lack of a strong sense of self.

Part of the problem seems to be his outwardly happy marriage. He had assumed at least one identity prior to marrying Bonny Cullen, that of the promising

EARTHLY POSSESSIONS **AND** *MORGAN'S PASSING*

young man in a yachting blazer; but after the wedding, whatever self he possessed had been lost in the Cullen identity. Owners of a string of successful hardware stores throughout Greater Baltimore, the Cullens gave Morgan Gower a beautiful home and a token job as manager of an older branch store. In short, they took away his actual identity while providing him with the time and money to compensate for the loss by playing different roles at his considerable leisure. Did he live in Charlotte Emory's straitened circumstances and tiny hometown—one so small that during an earlier escape effort, Saul knew she was registered at the Blue Moon Motel minutes after she checked in—Morgan could not be trying on different lives virtually at whim.[12] Likewise, the otherwise commendable understanding of Morgan's wife proves to be a liability: Bonny lets him do whatever he wishes instead of recognizing the serious identity crisis at the center of his elaborate game and helping him to integrate his true selfhood. Not part of the solution, Bonny Gower definitely is part of the problem.

Ironically, a central aspect of that selfhood would involve truly assuming the various roles that marriage to Bonny Cullen denies: those of husband, father, breadwinner, artist. Ensconced in a mansion full of women—his wife, seven daughters, his senile mother Louisa, and his sister Brindle (the latter two are "lunatics" [308, *288*])—Morgan has seen the raising of his children assumed by the ever-resourceful Bonny, while his creativity, finding no outlet in managing a hardware store, dovetails with his psychological need to pose as other people: though he can maintain only briefly his various assumed guises, he is always the consummate actor.

Hence his attraction to Emily and Leon Meredith. They too are creative individuals, but they can pursue their creative endeavors openly and purposefully, he as an actor, she as a puppeteer whose characters play out the roles that she herself is too timid to pursue: Princess, Beauty, Cinderella. More surprisingly, the frenetic Morgan is attracted to the Merediths' balanced family life (one husband, one wife, one child, no relatives) and their capacity to work together to earn their living, neither of which is evident in his own situation. Morgan responds strongly to the "streamlined" (22, *20*) quality of their lives and their occupations as traveling performers, though neither perception is quite accurate: he finds it difficult to accept that they acquire such mundane encumbrances as diaper service, a Volkswagen, a television, and new clothing, while they stress from the outset that their travels as itinerant puppeteers are actually quite limited: " 'You think we're some kind of transients,' she said, 'but we're not. We're legally married, and we live in a regular apartment with furniture. . . . [W]e're almost always home by night. We're never *shiftless*. You have the wrong idea' " (20–21, *18*).

But the fact remains that the qualities, real or otherwise, to which Morgan responds in the Merediths betoken the "true" Morgan Gower who had somehow become lost in the course of his marriage to Bonny Cullen. The true Morgan Gower does not want the chaos and disorder that surround him including, presumably, the masses of costumes and hats in his closets or the compulsion to keep taking on new identities. "I have an interest in order," Morgan unexpectedly reports, one that he had assumed—like Elizabeth Abbott and self-reliance in *The Clock Winder*—would come with the passage of time: "When I was a child, I thought order might come when my voice changed. Then I thought, no, maybe when I'm educated. At one point I thought I would be orderly if I could just once sleep with a woman" (140, *130*). Now in middle age, Morgan realizes he had fooled himself: he must actively find or generate order, and he sees in Emily order personified, right down to her sole "costume"—a leotard, a long wrap skirt, and ballet slippers. Stark in their simplicity and seemingly timeless ("they made fashion seem beside the point" [48, *45*]), these clothes are the embodiment of all that Morgan's true self desires. That true self initially leads him to want to step into Leon's own trademark costume (khaki trousers, white shirt, rust-colored corduroy jacket with the elbows worn); but eventually he steps into Leon's role as Emily's husband and even acquires his name. Ironically, in this final instance Morgan is not simply playing a role; rather, he is responding to necessity: Durwood Linthicum of the Holy Word Entertainment Troupe wants to hire Leon Meredith to work for him, and Morgan, with a new wife and baby boy to support, accedes to the demands of this second family. Though he does occasionally engage in role playing, including that of an accommodating mailman at the very end of the novel, Morgan Gower as Leon Meredith is finally a happy man, responsible to his loved ones while honoring his true self.

He had failed to honor it for most of his fifty-three years, as indeed had Charlotte Emory. In doing so, they had, in effect, not exercised their freedom; and the nature of freedom, plus the forces (external or otherwise) that undermine it, are central concerns of both novels.

Probably the most obvious external check on one's personal freedom is household clutter, although it is important to recognize that Tyler regards this domestic detrita as significant only to the extent that it reflects the relationships and responsibilities that impinge upon daily life. Morgan's home with Bonny is, of course, packed with "the particles of related people's unrelated worlds," including his daughters' booksacks, his wife's League of Women Voters leaflets, his mother's dog, his sister's jigsaw puzzles, and someone's lost cribbage board (26, 24). Even Morgan's car, in which little Gina is born, is a microcosm on wheels of his messy domestic life, including "schoolbooks and dirty socks and gym bloomers and rucked-up movie magazines" (11, 9). As noted, Morgan is attracted to Emily because of her streamlined self-sufficiency: she makes do with an all-purpose Swiss army knife, wears leotards because with them "she wouldn't need underwear" (79, 74), and creates her puppets in a stark room with a stepladder doubling as a chair. To Morgan, she seems to lead an uncluttered life and to have the freedom to move at a moment's notice—a freedom confirmed when she takes up jogging and trains herself to run five miles at a stretch. But the impedimenta of daily life is insidious: once Morgan moves into Emily's apartment, it too begins to acquire the clutter that characterized his home with Bonny—clutter that includes his mother, sister, and dog Harry. Even little Gina cannot tolerate it, opting to move with her father to Richmond, where he pursues a settled existence as a trainee banker. Not until Emily and Morgan realize that they have simply "transplanted all the mess from home" and need to "ditch [it] all" in order to survive (307–08, *287–88*) do they rid themselves of most of their impedimenta. They move into a trailer on the entertainment circuit; and though it is a crowded one—baby Joshua's Port-a-Crib takes up most of the bedroom—it is filled with things that they actually need and want. Were these objects to be transported to a house the size of Bonny's, they would leave most of it empty.

This stripped-down, functional existence would not be possible, however, without the departure of Louisa, Brindle, and Gina, a situation which suggests that it is other people who often serve as the most dramatic check on one's personal freedom. Morgan had admittedly felt "oppressed" by his mother's presence even in his old house (38, *35*), and he longed to be left behind alone at Bethany Beach after his dreaded, people-packed annual vacation: "Fall would come and he'd be buried under drifting threads of sand and a few brown leaves blown seaward. . . . He would finally have a chance to sort himself out. It was *people* who disarranged his life" (186, *173*).

It is a sentiment that would be appreciated readily by Charlotte Emory, whose freedom is likewise checked by household clutter and other people. It literally is difficult to walk in the Emory home. Her husband Saul had moved all the furniture from the home of his mother Alberta into Charlotte's house when he married her: "The house was overstuffed as it was, so [Saul] had to double things up: an end table in front of another end table, a second sofa backed against the first. It was crazy. Every piece of furniture had its shadow, a Siamese twin" (113, *100–01*). To further complicate matters, Charlotte's brother-in-law Linus carves doll furniture that mimics, in miniature, the clutter of her household: "on every tabletop there were other tables," and "each tiny surface bore its own accessories," including lamps with toothpaste caps for shades. "Entire roomfuls were grouped beneath the desk and under the piano" (161–62, *145*). Linus makes them specifically for Charlotte, a fact which suggests that, like Nora in Ibsen's play, she is essentially living in a doll house, a child's fantasy world that has no relation to the real world of adulthood. On some level Charlotte is aware

EARTHLY POSSESSIONS AND *MORGAN'S PASSING*

of this, but she is unable to determine how to change her life without disrupting those of the people who depend on her, including her husband, three brothers-in-law, daughter Catherine (who absorbed the identity of her imaginary friend Selinda), adopted son Jiggs, and assorted sinners from the mourner's bench at the Holy Basis Church who had nowhere else to go. After all, if Charlotte were to leave, who would make their breakfasts? But however passive she may be, she cannot ignore her desire for freedom, although it manifests itself in ways that are rarely constructive: she begins to move out Saul's mother's furniture piece by piece, until Saul discovers her betrayal; she yearns to take a "wilderness course" ("Learn to live on my own with no equipment. Cover great distances. In the desert and the Alps and such" [208, *187*]); she buys a pair of "excellent walking shoes" (42, *37*); and she acquires a $100 traveler's check. Clearly she wants not simply to travel but to escape; but as is signified by the facts that she forgets she even has the check and never does learn to drive, Charlotte is too overwhelmed by the things, people, and commitments in her life to translate her need for freedom into purposeful action. The best she can hope for is to be carried off.

Jake Simms proves to be the agent of her escape. Charlotte had been taken hostage while withdrawing money from the bank to leave Saul; but since she had half-heartedly tried to escape once before, in 1960, it seems clear that this thirty-five-year-old housewife, a hostage of her own existence and self-perception as much as of Jake Simms, probably would not have made good with her second escape attempt sixteen years later. She responds immediately to the opportunity that Jake has unwittingly provided: although she is understandably terrified of him at first, she also enters fully into the process of escape, nearly outdistancing him in their getaway and being seriously suspected by the police of being his accomplice rather than his victim. After all, to abandon one's husband and children is nearly as anti-social as to rob a bank. But she still is indeed a victim, and Charlotte submits to Jake as readily as she submitted to an earlier kidnapper, the refugee at the state fair's Beautiful Child Contest many years before. Acceding to other people's plans and expectations is an integral part of Charlotte's temperament. As Amos points out, "You're the kind who thinks tolerance is a virtue" (205, *185*).

True; but what further complicates matters is that the people to whom she so willingly accommodates herself are often themselves victims. The refugee became a kidnapper due to the psychological trauma of displacement during World War II. She mistakes little Charlotte for a child she had no choice but to abandon during her desperate trek, and she seeks to assuage her guilt: "'Say it,' she said. 'Do you forgive me?' [Charlotte] said, 'Sure'" (38, *33*). Jake Simms is likewise a victim, although his lack of freedom is ironic to the point of caricature. He feels that he is not being allowed to release Charlotte: "It ain't *me* keeping you, it's them. If they would quit hounding me then we could go our separate ways" (26, 22). He even feels that he achieved so little success as a bank robber simply because of someone else, an armed customer. Though he is pleased that his friend Oliver regards him as a "victim of impulse" (49, 43), he seems to feel more strongly that he is a victim of bad luck and unknown forces: "'It's circumstances, working against me,' said Jake. 'Like I told Oliver: I surely don't plan it like this. Events get out of my control'" (51, 45).

Even Morgan Gower, whose lifestyle would seem to be an endless indulgence of whimsy and freedom, is to some degree a victim of other victims. He poses as a physician to deliver the Merediths' baby simply because no one else is available to help the desperate couple; he poses as a cobbler to reassure a distraught woman whose Italian shoes are falling apart; and he poses as a mailman to calm an irate postal patron. "I often find myself giving a false impression," understates Morgan, but "It's not something I intend . . . It almost seems that other people conspire with me, push me into it." Further, they exacerbate the problem by being "so willing to believe me": "they'll believe me all the quicker if I tell them something disillusioning. I might say, for instance, that being a movie star is not what it's cracked up to be"—that, for example, the hot lights cause his make-up to run, leaving his collars perpetually soiled (128, *119*).[13]

Material objects and other people are not the only checks on freedom in these two novels. Without pressing the matter too far, Tyler suggests that both genetic factors and early environment are important elements. Emily Meredith, for example, apparently inherited her skill with puppets from her Aunt Mercer, something she did not realize until she attended the old woman's funeral. "Maybe it was something that was passed in the dark through the generations—the very thought of giving puppet shows, even. And here she imagined she'd come so far, lived such a different existence!" (221, *206*). This recognition is initially unsettling, and it leads her to respond more warmly to the attentions of Morgan.

Even he, however, seems the victim of a complex interaction of genes and early experience. His father had died a suicide, and Morgan is desperate to find out why. One reason he feels the compulsion to assume various identities is to prevent his own "interest in life" from "just thin[ning] to a trickle and dry[ing] up" (50, *47*): role-playing, in other words, reflects his conscious attempt to avoid his father's fate. Bonny, in contrast, does not see her husband's eccentricities as something he can control: "I wonder if there's even any point in blaming him. It's the way he *is*, right? It's in his genes," and she cites various male Gower ancestors whose offbeat behavior would help explain Morgan's (300, *280*). Tyler makes no effort to indicate which explanation is correct, thereby suggesting that all these factors are at

work, interacting in ways that are impossible to un-
ravel.

A final important check on personal freedom is the
burden of the past, yet another Hawthornesque element in Tyler's work. Charlotte Emory, of course,
seems crushed under the weight of personal and familial history. She is raising her family in the same house
in which she grew up, and her own mother grew up
there as well. The very thought oppresses her, and no
doubt she would respond warmly to Holgrave's suggestion in *The House of the Seven Gables* that each generation
should build its own houses and raze the old.[14] The
materials within Charlotte's home are likewise oppressive: the negatives of photographs of long-dead customers pile up in the studio, while her living room is packed
with her mother-in-law's furniture along with sixty
years' worth of theatrical clippings and costumes once
owned by Alberta's husband. No wonder Charlotte is
attracted to her brother-in-law Amos, a footloose bache-
lor who seemingly "carried no freight of past wrongs
and debts" (196, *176*). But she is incorrect in her perception of him: he is, in his way, as burdened as she, "hop-
ping around like something in a skillet" and unable to
hold a job or to pursue a worthwhile relationship because of his own past. For, contrary to Charlotte's positive impression of her, his mother Alberta had been a
terror, "pushy, clamorous, violent," a woman remembered for "taking over [her sons'] lives, meddling in
their brains, demanding a constant torrent of admira-

tion and gaiety" (167, *150–51*). And Saul hates her most of all: "It took Saul years and years to get as bitter as he is. He's come away from her in shreds; all of us have" (168, *151*). The furniture he insists upon retaining is the emblem not of love, but of guilt over hating his mother and of a painful past that he carries with him always.

Morgan Gower, too, feels the awful burden of the past, not only in the haunting memory of his father's suicide, but in the endless vacation photographs that never seem to change from one year to the next. They simply pile up, along with everything else: "Aren't we all sitting on stacks of past events? And not every level is neatly finished off, right? Sometimes a lower level bleeds into an upper level" (143, *133*). But the very phenomenon of bleeding holds out the possibility of hope, both for Morgan and for the other characters as well. As Justine Peck had eventually discovered in *Searching for Caleb*, one need not be the helpless victim of genes, upbringing, or circumstances: one can *choose* positive elements to accept and nurture, while downplaying or selectively forgetting the negative. To succeed, this process depends upon cultivating particular attitudes and shifting one's point of view in the hope of eventually attaining a kind of psychological compromise or spiritual balance. Household clutter, for example, need not be physically burdensome or emotionally oppressive. Emily Meredith absolutely revels in the clutter brought to her apartment by Morgan: she "loved it all" (289,

EARTHLY POSSESSIONS AND *MORGAN'S PASSING*

270). The trailer in which they eventually live is also filled with objects, but they all are things that they truly need or want. As Emily comes to realize, "you could draw vitality from mere objects" (289, *270*), a positive attitude that reveals the ludicrousness of Charlotte Emory's determination to rid her home of literally everything: "After all, did we really need to write at desks, walk on rugs?" (115, *102*). Perhaps more dramatically, though it at first distresses her, Emily eventually is delighted that she has inherited from her aunt a skill that she loves. What one acquires need not be a burden; it may be a gift.

Closely aligned with this, the image of bleeding levels suggests both continuity and separateness, both stasis and change. Emily is not Aunt Mercer; she is a separate being; but wherever she goes, and whatever she does, a part of her beloved aunt will always be with her—just as her daughter Gina will always have the distinctive Aunt Mercer nose with which she was born. These realizations enable Emily to allow Gina to move back with her father, as the child wishes, for as mother and daughter they can never be totally separate from each other. This paradigm of continuity and separateness, stasis and change, is evident even at the level of clothing: Emily always wears a leotard, but it is not always the same one. She has bought many "replacement leotards" over the years (307, *288*).

For change is an inevitable aspect of life; and although Tyler's characters have difficulty accepting this at first—witness Morgan's inability to deal with his daughter's getting married, or Charlotte's pretending that she's only substituting for her photographer-father for seventeen years—they do work their way painfully to this plateau of thought. Where it proves most essential is in their attitudes towards quotidian realities, especially in the domestic sphere.

Enough has been said to suggest the clutter and confusion of the households in both *Earthly Possessions* and *Morgan's Passing*, and Tyler's characters have an understandable urge to abandon these worlds that run so counter to the needs of the self. But, like it or not, daily living, and in particular the raising of children, requires that one deal with matters like food, clothing, and housing. Simply to run away is just not feasible. What these characters truly need, therefore, is to find some sort of workable compromise, some way of dealing with the fact that life is, as Morgan's son-in-law phrases it, "part bed, part grocery-shopping" (272, 254). Certainly Bonny Gower recognizes this, maintaining that it's fine for Morgan to wear all those costumes, but someone still has to locate a laundry that can handle ostrich plumes. Most of the characters, however, either do not realize this, or have difficulty accepting it. As a result, too often they resort to either endlessly indulging the self ("bed") or passively acceding to the demands of others ("grocery-shopping") or fooling themselves into thinking that they need not acknowledge either.

EARTHLY POSSESSIONS AND *MORGAN'S PASSING*

For example, it is painfully easy for Charlotte Emory to accept her lot in life, to tolerate someone else's furniture on top of her own and to acquiesce quietly as her husband brings home abandoned babies and displaced sinners. It is even more easy for the members of her husband's congregation to abdicate any responsibility for themselves or for others. Dr. Sisk, for example, tired of the quotidian reality of Vicks VapoRub and stethoscopes, had contemplated suicide, but then had taken the advice of a preacher:

"Recommended I give my life to Christ, instead. Well, I liked the way he put it. I mean, just to hand my life *over*. Isn't that true, my dear," he said to me [i.e., Charlotte].

"Well," I said, "but you still have income tax and license renewals."

"Beg pardon?"

"Still have bank statements and dental appointments and erroneous bills," I said. "If it were all that easy, don't you think I'd long ago have handed *my* life over?"

Dr. Sisk sat down and started pulling at his nose. (160–61, *144*)

These are the very quotidian realities that Morgan Gower has been able to leave to his wife Bonny on the homefront and to his clerk Butkins at the hardware store. But under the pressure of Emily's unexpected pregnancy, Morgan comes to a new appreciation of Butkins, who falls into a kind of trance between customers:

Perhaps he was thinking of his wife. She had some slow, creeping illness . . . She was no longer able to walk. And the child who died had been struck by a hit-and-run driver. Morgan remembered the funeral. He wondered how Butkins endured it, where he found the strength to open his eyes every morning and dress himself and force down a little food and set out for the hardware store. He must feel nothing but contempt for Morgan. But when Butkins came out of his trance and found Morgan's eyes on him, he only gave his gentle smile. (269, 251)

This "gentle smile" squares exactly with new attitudes that Morgan is suddenly experiencing as a result of Emily's pregnancy: he flings one of his favorite hats to the ground, recognizing that it is no different from the firemen's helmets and Indian headdresses he had worn as a child ("What a farce! How ridiculous!" [268, 250]), and he comes to see that Emily's pregnancy is neither a tragedy nor a complication, but an "assignment" to be accepted responsibly:

He began to see the situation from another angle. An assignment had been given him. Someone's life, a small set of lives, had been placed in the palm of his hand. Maybe he would never have any more purpose than this: to accept the assignment gracefully, lovingly, and do the best he could with it. (264, *246*)

He decides, like Butkins, to endure, and by the end of the novel he is a contented man. The old Morgan Gower is dead, has "passed," as confirmed by the obituary Bonny placed in the newspaper. The new Morgan Gower is working alongside Emily and, unlike his first marriage, is actually raising his child. Like Justine and Duncan Peck, they are able to combine both travel (not escape) and home (not prison) by working with an entertainment troupe.[15]

Meanwhile, Charlotte Emory returns home. *Earthly Possessions* is not, as censorious reviewers would have it, a circular novel which accomplishes nothing, shows no growth on the part of its characters, and wastes the time of anyone foolish enough to read it.[16] Nor is there anything tinny about the ending of the novel: Charlotte is not, like Dorothy, intoning "There's no place like home," nor is this "sleeping" princess awakening to what she fondly believes is a perfect, fairy tale world (196, *176*). The road ahead of her will be, like the route of the Founder's Day parade, a minefield of horse droppings, "great beehives of manure" (147, *131*). One can either step smartly around them, like the majorettes, or slog through like the determined soldiers. Ultimately the point is to keep marching. Charlotte now knows that she must replace her customary passivity with endurance; that perhaps, with time and effort, her mar-

riage will strengthen and her husband will evolve, like
his Biblical namesake, from Saul to the more clear-
sighted Paul; and that "Keep on Truckin'" truly was a
"sign" (28, 24) for her—a sign not to run, but to endure.[17]

Notes

1. Nicholas Delbanco spoke for many in his review of *Earthly
Possessions*, maintaining that "the wheels are a touch too audibly
clicking, and inspiration seems second-hand. . . . [T]he book is pro-
grammatic and the program feels over-rehearsed. Still, anyone who
wrote the splendid *Celestial Navigation* and *Searching for Caleb* should
be allowed to take a breather." Even so, Delbanco hoped that "its
author, next time, . . . will once more be fully engaged" ([rev. of
Earthly Possessions], *New Republic* 176 [28 May 1977]: 36).

Reviews of *Morgan's Passing* were less kind. Eva Hoffman wrote
that the characters are "too lethargic, too passive, and the novel remains suspended in a chilly, murky, ozone-thin limbo—a bit as if
Flannery O'Connor were writing in a fog. Without an exploration that
would make the characters more familiar, and without a perspective
that would make their estrangement significant, Anne Tyler is left
with a story about weirdness—and weirdness, as a novelistic subject,
is simply not enough" ("When the Fog Never Lifts," *Saturday Review*
7 [15 March 1980]: 39). A. G. Mojtabai argued that the problem was
"Anne Tyler's relation to Morgan": "She seems at once too casually
fond of Morgan to subject him to a truly loving, yet deeply probing
scrutiny, and too beguiled by his disorderly charm to give us any
outside perspective on him" ("A State of Continual Crisis," *New York
Times Book Review* [23 March 1980]: 14). Ironically, *Morgan's Passing*

EARTHLY POSSESSIONS AND *MORGAN'S PASSING*

was the first Tyler book to be honored: it earned her a nomination for the National Book Critics Circle Award for 1981, as well as the Janet Heidinger Kafka Prize, presented by the University of Rochester for outstanding achievement in fiction by an American woman.

2. "One summer, when I was working on Morgan, carrying him around, it just seemed there was one emergency after another, one child or the other, it was always something happening, and I could see Morgan in his broad-brimmed hat, fading away. It took me a week's work to get him back, but then he perked up" (Wendy Lamb, "An Interview with Anne Tyler," *Iowa Journal of Literary Studies* 3 [1981]: 62). Tyler discusses her difficulties with the creation of *Morgan's Passing* in "Still Just Writing," in Janet Sternburg, ed., *The Writer on Her Work* (New York: Norton, 1980): 3–16.

3. "After *Earthly Possessions,* I wrote a novel that I ditched. A year's work, out the door. . . . I sent it to my agent, who didn't like it; so I said, don't send it out [to possible publishers]. Now if I had really liked it myself, nothing would have stopped me. The problem was that it was boring." As a result of this crisis, "I'm not as confident now": "This new novel, Morgan's [sic], is giving me a hell of a time" (quoted in Lamb 60).

4. John Updike makes the point that, with the arrival of Mindy, "the Shakespearean ambience of dark comedy turns Spenserian; we are travelling in an allegory, and Love (Mindy) points to the Grail" ("Loosened Roots," *The New Yorker* 53 [6 June 1977]: 130).

5. Frank W. Shelton, "The Necessary Balance: Distance and Sympathy in the Novels of Anne Tyler," *Southern Review* 20 (Autumn 1984): 855. Eva Hoffman observes that roughly half-way through the novel, as its "absurdist perplexities are neither clarified nor deepened, [the reader's] curiosity turns into exasperation" (38), while Edmund Fuller, although claiming to like Morgan, admits that "I grow tired of him sometimes" ("Micawber as a Hardware Store Manager," *The Wall Street Journal* 195 [21 April 1980]: 26). One may argue, however, that the style of the novel is ideally suited to a study of a man whose life is in chaos. As Peter Grier observes, in *Morgan's Passing* "the charac-

UNDERSTANDING ANNE TYLER

ters and plot seem to be stuck together with baling wire and chewing gum," as if the book were "a jalopy with a dirty carburetor. . . . But in the end, the book plops you at its promised destination as surely as if it were a purring limousine" ("Bright Novel That Overstretches Credibility," *Christian Science Monitor* 72 [14 April 1980]: B9).

6. Frank W. Shelton declines even to discuss it in his essay on Tyler's books, dismissing it as "a runaway housewife novel" (857). Several critics identified this genre as characteristic of the new feminist era: "the leave-taking housewife has become a cliché of current fiction" (Katherine Bouton, [rev. of *Earthly Possessions*], *Ms.* 6 [August 1977]: 35). Tyler herself believes that the novel is generally misunderstood to be "another Unhappy Housewife Leaves Home book, which was the last thought in my mind." Rather, she regards it "as the work of somebody entering middle age, beginning to notice how the bags and baggage of the past are weighing her down, and how much she values them" (Mary Ellen Brooks, "Anne Tyler," in *The Dictionary of Literary Biography*, Vol. 6: *American Novelists Since World War II* [Detroit: Gale Research, 1980]: 344, 343). Tyler further admits that it "was written before I realized what the pattern was—that a relationship as bizarre as a bank robber and hostage could become a bickering familiar relationship" (Marguerite Michaels, "Anne Tyler, Writer 8:05 to 3:30," *New York Times Book Review* [8 May 1977]: 43).

As for *Morgan's Passing,* A. G. Mojtabai argues that "this might have been the story of a midlife crisis, a familiar tale, with steady, reliable associations, however tormented; but Miss Tyler chose instead to depict an unfamiliar state of continual crisis, a condition for which there exist no charts or manuals ready to hand" (33).

7. Updike 130.

8. Walter Sullivan, "The Insane and the Indifferent Walker Percy and Others," *Sewanee Review* 86 (Winter 1978): 156. Much of Sullivan's dislike of Jake is on moral grounds: "I take the position, quaint as it is, that robbing banks is a crime and stealing a sin and people ought to keep their hands off other people's money" (156). Tyler herself disagrees: "I like every one of my characters; this is very

important to me. My mother is shocked by this. She says, 'How can you *like* someone like Jake (the bank robber in *Earthly Possessions*)?' But what I like is a sense of character, however spiky or difficult the person may be" (quoted in Lamb 61).

9. Anne G. Jones, "Home at Last, and Homesick Again: The Ten Novels of Anne Tyler," *The Hollins Critic* 23 (April 1986): 7–8. Gilberto Perez misunderstands the significance of the two voices, arguing that "in a retrospective account . . . we feel cheated unless we get some sense all along that the narrator knows how things will turn out" ("Narrative Voices," *Hudson Review* 30 [Winter 1977–78]: 612). Though Charlotte knows the facts of what happens to her, she does not know their implications until the end of her kidnapping ordeal—and the end of the novel.

10. Robert Towers argues that "twentieth-century psychology has largely tainted the comfortable Victorian enjoyment of eccentric characters in fiction. . . . Today readers and writers alike can accommodate any degree of weirdness, neurosis, perversion, or madness but tend to jib at the droll, the quirky, the harmlessly odd." Only two writers this century, according to Towers, "have successfully evaded the ban on colorfully eccentric characters," V. S. Pritchett and Anne Tyler ([rev. of *Morgan's Passing*], *New Republic,* 182 [22 March 1980]: 28). Edmund Fuller of *The Wall Street Journal* likens Morgan to Dickens's Mr. Micawber and W. C. Fields (26), while Thomas M. Disch notes that "Not since [John Irving's] Garp have I come across a character in a recent novel who is at once so plausibly flawed and so improbably lovable" ("The Great Impostor," *Washington Post Book World* 10 [16 March 1980]: 5). David Kubal suggests Morgan's kinship with two characters created by Saul Bellow, Henderson and Herzog ([rev. of *Morgan's Passing*], *Hudson Review* 33 [Autumn 1980]: 440).

11. Two critics who make this mistake are the anonymous reviewer for *The Virginia Quarterly Review* 56 (Autumn 1980): 139; and Mary F. Robertson, "Medusa Points & Contact Points," in Catherine Rainwater and William J. Scheick, eds., *Contemporary American Women*

UNDERSTANDING ANNE TYLER

Writers: Narrative Strategies (Lexington: UP of Kentucky, 1985): 122 *et passim.*

12. Morgan "can play and be accepted in his roles because he lives in Baltimore, a large city where the contact between individuals tends to be fleeting and a role can be sustained for the short period of time necessary" (Shelton 856). The inherited wealth of Morgan's wife also facilitates his role playing. Unfortunately without probing the implications of this situation, Paul Gray does acknowledge it in the title of his review of *Morgan's Passing:* "The Rich Are Different," *Time* 115 (17 March 1980): 31.

13. Tyler herself admits a certain kinship to Morgan, noting that her novel "deals with a situation I've been fascinated by for most of my life, and one which probably is not unrelated to being a writer: the inveterate imposter [sic], who is unable to stop himself from stepping into other people's worlds" (quoted in Brooks 344). She notes further that Morgan "has a terrible tendency to step into other people's lives" (quoted in Lamb 59), a phrase that echoes the title of her 1976 account of her work as a writer: "Because I Want More Than One Life," *Washington Post* (15 August 1976), Sec. G: 1, 7. Morgan's explanation of the incapacity of either Clorox or Wisk to clean an actor's stained collar calls to mind Tyler's comment that in writing a novel, "You set out to tell an untrue story and you try to make it believable, even to yourself. Which calls for details; any good lie does. I'm quicker to believe I was once a circus aerialist if I remember that just before every performance, I used to dip my hands in a box of chalk powder that smelled like clean, dry cloth being torn" ("Because I Want" G1).

14. Arguing that we are "slaves" to "the Past" ("It lies upon the Present like a giant's dead body!"), Holgrave theorizes that "If each generation were allowed and expected to build its own houses, that single change, comparatively unimportant in itself, would imply almost every reform which society is now suffering for" (Chap. 12).

15. Several commentators have noted that "Hints of myth, of fairytale, abound in the novel . . . Morgan is a protean figure, a shape-

shifter, Emily an unawakened princess or a princess in rags, Leon a glowering beast [hence his name], a truculent prince" (Towers 31). One may add that, to a large extent, Morgan lives out the fantasy of so many middle-aged American males: he leaves his boring managerial job, marries a woman young enough to be his daughter, fathers a male child, and unloads his impossible mother and sister on his ever-accommodating ex-wife, whose personal fortune obviates the need for alimony payments. When matters work out so tidily for all concerned, Tyler runs the risk of undercutting most of the serious statements she is trying to make.

16. Walter Sullivan argues that Charlotte "goes back home with neither herself nor her situation much altered by this silly adventure." Consequently, "The hours spent in reading *Earthly Possessions* leave you no wiser than when you began. You wind up empty-handed" (156–57). John Updike admits that Tyler's "one possible weakness" is "a tendency to leave the reader just where she found him . . . or, as 'Earthly Possessions' would have it, the end of travelling is to return" (130). Less charitably, Anatole Broyard, describing Charlotte as "a woman on the run from boredom toward an empty ambiguity," claims that "she merely rolls around until she stops" ("Tyler, Tracy and Wakefield," *New York Times Book Review* [8 May 1977]: 12).

17. Robertson 136.

CHAPTER EIGHT

Dinner at the Homesick Restaurant

Anne Tyler is candid about what she was trying to accomplish in her ninth novel, *Dinner at the Homesick Restaurant* (1982): "I think what I was doing was saying, 'Well, all right, I've joked around about families long enough; let me tell you now what I really believe about them.'"[1] What she "really believes" is nicely conveyed by the word "homesick." As various commentators have pointed out, its meaning is multifaceted. At one level, "homesick" can mean "sick for home," longing nostalgically for the warmth and security associated with the locale and group with which one is most familiar, and perhaps even emphasizing selectively one's positive memories to such an extreme degree that the remembered "home" is essentially a fantasy. On another level, "homesick" can mean "sick *of* home," yearning to break free of the strictures which are the underside of that security while not denying either the attractiveness or the value of it. On a final level, "homesick" can mean "sick *from* home""—psychologically debilitated as the result of "home" not just in the sense of

186

one's childhood domicile, but more obtusely in the sense of the traumatic experiences, dubious parental examples, and even the genetic legacy that are so often visited upon hapless offspring.

Each of these three points on the spectrum of homesickness is embodied in the life of one of the Tull children. There is Ezra, whose repeated attempts to have a "real family dinner" (92, *90*) convey his yearning to capture the happiness, real or otherwise, embodied in the idea of the Tull home. And there is Jenny, who attempts to create a separate life for herself as a successful pediatrician and much-married woman while not quite relinquishing her ties to the Tull family circle. And finally there is Cody, who in his angry determination to reject what he recalls as a miserable homelife only replicates the more vigorously the very qualities he seeks to escape. The three Tull children's various kinds of homesickness are conveyed metaphorically through their own homes in adulthood: Ezra never moves out of the Baltimore row house in which he spent his childhood; after college and medical school in Pennsylvania, Jenny buys a large house away from Ezra and mother Pearl, but still within Baltimore; and Cody refuses either to stay in the city or to establish a permanent home, simply renting a series of stridently un-homelike houses throughout the United States. As they are situated away from the Tull home in a series of concentric circles, the three children retain their emotional orbits around the senior Tulls—both the always-present Pearl and the never-present Beck, their personal "black hole"[3]—long after they have reached middle age.

To convey the disparate levels of homesickness experienced by each Tull child and, concomitantly, to explain how each child arrived at that level and responds to it, Tyler presents her material in her most technically complex novel to that time. To be sure, *Dinner at the Homesick Restaurant* owes much to the precedent of *Celestial Navigation*, in which each chapter is presented in the first person from one character's point of view (the exception, of course, is Jeremy's third-person narratives), but in *Dinner* Tyler has improved upon the model. She avoids using the first person, which was responsible for the "sometimes jolting and mechanical transitions" between the alternating chapters in *Earthly Possessions*.[4] Further, she opens the book with a chapter from the point of view not of one of the children, but of their mother, Pearl Cody Tull. As a dying woman, Pearl is casting a backward glance on her life, less out of nostalgia than out of the impulse to relocate the young Pearl Cody in diaries and photographs—the old self which, like that of Morgan Gower, had somehow become misplaced in adulthood and marriage. Though there is nothing strikingly original about using a deathbed as a novelistic structural device, Tyler does play with the convention to good effect by presenting the story proper not through Pearl's recollections (although these recur in, for example, Chapter Six) but rather those of her children; in effect, she both uses and under-

DINNER AT THE HOMESICK RESTAURANT

cuts the convention of the deathbed, in much the way that William Faulkner uses it in *As I Lay Dying* (1930).[5] Each chapter of Tyler's novel is essentially a self-contained short story, told from the perspective of one character, and ranging readily from present to past. The overall effect, argues Anne G. Jones, is that "the reader is schooled in caring for each flawed character. So the effect of those lucid revelatory scenes is to produce, in the reader, the deepest sense so far in Tyler of irony that is both understood and felt."[6] At the same time, the rapid time movement permits Tyler "to juxtapose past and present and thus to convey the vision—that she has always had—of the past not as a continuum but as layers of still, vivid memories." This, in turn, "allows Tyler to show more fully than ever the essential subjectivity of the past."[7] And to further underscore the irony and subjectivity, Tyler also includes chapters told from the point of view of Cody's teen-aged son Luke (Chapter Eight) and from the perspective of an omniscient narrator (Chapter Ten). As a result, the reader comes to know the Tull children even better than they know themselves: multiple points of view—including that of Luke Tull, technically an objective outsider albeit a blood relative—expose the sometimes frightening inner workings of a family and its impact on the adult lives of three individuals raised within it. As John Updike has written, Tyler has never before shown, "so searchingly and grimly, . . . the violence, ironies, and estrangements within a household, as the easy wounds given dependent flesh refuse to heal and instead grow into lifelong purposes. A bitter *narrowness* of life is disclosed through all the richness of detail as the decades accumulate, to claustrophobic and sad effect."[8] And yet, ultimately, that is not Tyler's primary concern. Rather, she probes the different kinds of homesickness that, rather unexpectedly, emerge from this sort of family situation while seeking to determine the inner resources, the attitudes, and the strategies that enable the three Tull children to become functional adults *despite* their childhood home. And they are functional, albeit in dramatically different ways.

The case of Cody Tull is probably the most problematic, largely because his homesickness is of the third type: he is spiritually "sick" as the result of his early home life. The family troublemaker, Cody seems to be at cross-purposes with everyone. True to form, Tyler declines to attribute his crusty temperament unequivocally to his childhood upbringing. Pearl tells him, for example, "You've been mean since the day you were born" (64), but there is ample evidence to suggest that Cody's personality problems have more to do with Pearl's upbringing of him than she is wont to admit. It was because of Cody's near-fatal attack of the croup when he was a baby in 1931 that Pearl resolved to have "extra" children (2, 4) as spares lest he should die—an impulse that, in its twisted way, suggests how much Pearl actually loved Cody. Unfortunately it also, ironically, set her up for the financial and emotional burden of raising three children alone—a burden which turns her, by her own admission, into "an angry sort of mother," one "continually on edge" (18, *19*). But Cody seems unable to comprehend either that Pearl loves him, or that her abusive outbursts resulted not from hatred of him but from the frustration of not being able to provide for him properly—and from the horrific realization that "everyone I love depends on me! I'm afraid I'll do something wrong" (63).

So Cody frantically spends a lifetime trying to win the motherly love he already has. As a child, he enacts "The Mortgage Overdue" with her (55). As an adolescent, he engineers scenarios in which Pearl's more favored son, Ezra, appears to be an incompetent, a drunk, a pervert—and in which Cody, by contrast, seems angelic. As an adult, he buys her the Baltimore row house which she has rented for years. But Cody's motives are always warped: he always is trying to buy her affection, to outmaneuver the non-maneuvering Ezra. Even his own son Luke recognizes, as Cody does not, that the bus ticket he bought for Pearl when he was seventeen was intended less to give her a much-welcomed vacation visit to her old friend Emmaline than to get her out of town during Ezra's birthday. Her refusal to accept the gift did not mean that she loved Ezra more, or that she would have gone had it been Cody's birthday instead. "You haven't the faintest idea what I'm trying to get across," declares Cody to Luke (225–26, *220*), but in fact the boy knows better than his father the distortions in

Cody's mind. To a certain extent, Cody is indeed the "bad son" in the ancient pattern of "good son/bad son" (189, *185*), one evident previously in Tyler's depiction of Caleb and Daniel Peck. But as in *Searching for Caleb,* she modifies the paradigm: she raises it to new heights and infuses it with greater complexity by arguing that the "bad" son is not bad but troubled. A "cuticle chewer" (135, *133*) well into middle age, Cody does what he does out of a bizarre brew of guilt, fear, and love.

For Cody blames himself for the departure of his father, Beck Tull. "Was it something I said? Was it something I did? Was it something I didn't do, that made you go away?" (47). None of the above; but Cody the efficiency expert is so determined to see the world reductively as a logical place of patterns and order, of cause and effect, that he has managed to convince himself that he is personally responsible for the one event that has reduced his mother to the desperate "Sweeney Meanie" (44, *45*) who is periodically inclined to "rampages" (49) of verbal and physical abuse directed against the children she loves, and that has left himself and his siblings the helpless victims both of their mother's rages and the world. It is a heavy burden for an adolescent to bear, and it warps Cody's emotional development. Determined never again to be out of control of a situation, he orients his life towards winning and dominating. He becomes an indefatigable Monopoly player, enjoying seeing the others lose as much as he enjoys winning—even if it requires cheating. It is a pattern he continues into adulthood, relishing the idea of having "the great, almighty Tanner Corporation" in his "power" simply because his father Beck had once worked for the firm (93, *92*), and pursuing Ruth Spivey precisely because she already belongs to Ezra: "What he liked was the competition, the hope of emerging triumphant from a neck-and-neck struggle with Ezra, his oldest enemy." It does not even bother him that "one of the contestants [Ezra] didn't even know he *was* a contestant" (154, *151–52*). What matters is that he wins Ruth from Ezra; but, as with his concerted efforts to win the love of a mother he terms "a raving, shrieking, unpredictable witch" (301, *294*), Cody's motives are unclear even to him.

For by obtaining Ruth, Cody is—once again, in a "sick" way—expressing not envy or hatred, but love for his brother Ezra.[9] Indeed, he had dropped an earlier girlfriend because she had criticized his brother: "she really hadn't understood Ezra; she hadn't appreciated what he was all about" (169, *166*). That Cody recognizes his love for his brother only sporadically—just a few pages earlier he had fantasized about shooting Ezra through the heart—does not change the fact that his motives are not malicious.

Cody's love, fear, and guilt help explain his immense success as an efficiency expert. Part of his motivation is a desire for cash. As he works his way from a Pontiac to a Cadillac to a Mercedes, Cody does seem to

place an inordinate emphasis on money, but it is important to remember that he values it primarily as a means
of obtaining control over life events. After all, had Beck
continued to support his family properly, the over-
wrought Pearl would have been less inclined to periodic
rampages, while his childhood memories would not
have been redolent of "only poverty and loneliness,"
of toys unbought and parties missed (21, 22). But less
obvious than the money-based control is the fact that
being an efficiency expert involves dealing with time:
"Time is my obsession," admits Cody, "not to waste it,
not to lose it. . . . If only Einstein were right and time
were a kind of river you could choose to step into at any
place along the shore" (228, 223). More than anything,
Cody would love to travel in a time machine: "It
wouldn't much matter to me where. Past or future: just
out of my time" (229, 223). That is, he would love to
visit the future, where theoretically all could be fine—
and he would love to re-visit the past, not because he
liked it, but because he could conceivably change it. As
Mary J. Elkins observes, "if one could manage time, one
could step into anywhere necessary and fix whatever
had gone wrong."[10] By further implication, Cody hates
the present, hates what the unfixable past has done to
him; but he is incapable of finding a way out of his
spiritual conundrum. As his purchase of a forty-acre
farm near Baltimore suggests, deep down Cody truly
does want to remain near the family that he loves, and
truly does want to establish a "real" home just as Ezra

DINNER AT THE HOMESICK RESTAURANT

wants a "real" family dinner. But instead he travels about the country, paying only brief visits to Baltimore and renting such un-homey houses as the "raw brick cube" in Illinois (183, *179*). Unable to honor his deepest wishes, Cody is indeed "sick" as a result of home; and although no one senses this more than he, he cannot change.

Somewhat better able to handle the situation is Cody's sister Jenny. Not part of the "good son/bad son" paradigm, she exists in a sort of gray area. She too remembers painful events from her childhood, including dreams in which her mother dragged her "out of hiding as the Nazis tramped up the stairs; accused her of sins and crimes that had never crossed Jenny's mind. Her mother told her, in an informative and considerate tone of voice, that she was raising Jenny to eat her" (70). But with the exception of her anorexia, traditionally a young woman's bid to exert control over her life, Jenny responds to childhood trauma quite differently from Cody. For one thing, she marries thrice, each time separating herself further away from her childhood self. By the end of the novel she is "Dr. Jenny Marie Tull Baines Wiley St. Ambrose" (191, *187*), the young Jenny Tull barely detectable in the series of accumulated identities. Her policy of separation from Pearl is also physical. Even before her marriage to Harley Baines, she had consciously avoided going home on school vacations, for "whenever Jenny returned [home], she was dampened almost instantly by the atmosphere of the house . . . It was like a respiratory ailment; on occasion, she believed she might be smothering" (84, 83), telltale symptoms for a woman whose own patients suffer most often from "Mother-itis" (282, 276). Further, Jenny had always wanted to practice medicine "in a medium-sized city, preferably not too far from a coast. (She liked knowing she could get out anytime. . . .)" (83, 82). The impulse to escape from her childhood home is clearly evident; but the city she happens to pick is, of all places, her hometown of Baltimore. Sick of home, Jenny runs—but not too far. For being sick of home does not imply a denial of its value or its appeal; and after her peak of rejection during young womanhood, Jenny comes to appreciate her early life as she gets older.

Several factors facilitate the cultivation of her conciliatory attitude of appreciation. For one thing, Jenny is temperamentally similar to her mother. However cruel Pearl may have been to her, Jenny at some level understood her because she is so much like her. Both have an inner core of strength: Jenny, one learns, "was not capable of being destroyed by love" (113, 111), much as her mother, despite her frantic behavior after Beck's departure, retained a "true, interior self" that was "enormous, larger than life, powerful. Overwhelming" (276, 270). Further, Jenny married her first husband for the same reason her spinster mother had married Beck Tull. Pearl wed Beck because he made her feel "reckless and dashing" (5, 6), while as for Jenny, "What appealed to her . . . was the *angularity* of the situation—

the mighty leap into space with someone she hardly knew" (90, *89*). Further, Harley Baines was just as obsessively orderly as Pearl, arranging his schoolbooks "by height and blocks of color" (102, *100*). Jenny's ill-considered marriage to Harley is thus an odd tribute to her mother even as it seems an escape from her, much as Cody's stealing Ruth from Ezra is, in a twisted way, a tribute to the brother he loves.

Even Jenny's career is both a way of dissociating herself from her mother and of acknowledging their kinship. As a physician, Dr. Jenny Tull is educationally and socioeconomically well beyond Pearl; and yet, as a pediatrician, Jenny is being a kind of surrogate mother to hundreds of children. She is able to act out the motherly impulses that she rarely detected in Pearl, a woman so exhausted by overwork and worry that she resorted to suppers out of tin cans. In part, then, Jenny's career is a means of compensating for the lack of mothering she received; but it is also a tribute to the little mothering that she did have—something that does not become clear to her until a crisis while she was in medical school. Evidently Jenny suffered a nervous breakdown while attempting to juggle both her coursework and the raising of her daughter Becky, by second husband Sam Wiley. Jenny is enough like her mother to resort to child abuse: "She slammed Becky's face into her Peter Rabbit dinner plate and gave her a bloody nose. She yanked a handful of her hair. All of her childhood returned to her: her mother's blows and slaps and curses, her mother's pointed fingernails digging into Jenny's arm, her mother shrieking 'Guttersnipe! Ugly little rodent!' . . ." (214, *209*). But Jenny is different enough from her mother to be receptive to outside help from the unlikeliest of sources, Pearl herself. A loving grandmother, Pearl takes excellent care of little Becky, reading to her repeatedly from the book that Jenny (and Anne Tyler, incidentally[11]) had loved as a child: *The Little House.* Seeing the interaction between Pearl and Becky reminds Jenny that her mother had patiently read her that book many times when she was a little girl—that, in fact, her childhood had been far more happy than the vividly-remembered, isolated incidents of abuse had led her to believe.

Suddenly realizing that she had been perceiving herself, her childhood, and her mother incorrectly, Jenny consciously resolves to learn "how to make it through life on a slant. She was trying to lose her intensity" (217, *212*)—the one quality she has most obviously acquired, whether by example or inherited temperament, from her mother. " 'You've changed,' her mother said (all intensity herself). 'You've grown so different, Jenny'" (217, *212*), and the changes are deliberate and conscious. Part of that change involves admitting that she can never find the "innocent, protective marriage" of her youthful dreams (80, *79*), a search that had led her directly to Harley Baines, a man whose idea of "protection" was to dictate her weight. Dramatically modifying her conception of the perfect spouse, Jenny eventually chooses Joe St. Ambrose, an abandoned father who needs *her* protection both for his easy-going self and his brood of children. She installs her new family in the immense house she had bought years before, a purchase made almost as if her subconscious had forced her to act upon what she had not at that time been able to articulate: that to be sick of home does not mean the complete rejection of it. The de facto head of her burgeoning household, Jenny comes to respond to her career, husband, daughter, and many stepchildren in a manner that is lovingly relaxed: unlike Pearl, who so obsessively sealed shut her house "as if for a hurricane" (15, *16*), Jenny is hardly ruffled by the fact that her third-floor bathtub drains "through the dining room ceiling" (196, *192*). Though her newly developed strategy of going through life "on a slant" has its price—she tends too readily to dismiss with jokes the troubles of her stepson Slevin—Jenny still stands as "a compelling example of a character's ability to outgrow a destructive background."[12]

Ezra, in contrast, is so preoccupied with the idea of his childhood home that he literally refuses to leave it, continuing to occupy his old room well into middle age. For if Cody's recollection of childhood was uniformly negative, Ezra's recollection is positive. Cody remembers Pearl as violent: "She slammed us against the wall and called us scum and vipers, said she wished us dead, shook us till our teeth rattled, screamed in our faces." Ezra, however, begs to differ: "It wasn't like that":

"You're going to deny it?" Cody asked him.
"No, but she wasn't *always* angry. Really she was angry very seldom, only a few times, widely spaced, that happened to stick in your mind."
Cody felt drained. (301, *294–95*)

Ezra urges Cody to "think of the other side" (302, *295*), a selective perception that has made him want to stay always with Pearl. But Ezra's attitude is not, as it might seem at first glance, the one that Tyler herself would advocate: to focus only on the good is, in its way, as distortive as to focus only on the bad, and the price Ezra has paid for his lifelong homesickness is minimal personal growth. Even in middle age he seems childlike, "a tourist on a female planet" (134, *132*). Incapable of forming permanent relationships with women of his own age, he is oddly accepting when Cody steals away Ruth Spivey: "What does it matter why he did it? He did it, that's all" (173, *170*). Determined to go through life "as a liquid"—Cody did so "as a rock" (169, *166*)—Ezra adjusts passively to whatever life hands him. After all, he still has his mother—an attachment so complete that when she lies dying, Ezra gives up on his own life. Finding a lump he presumes to be malignant, Ezra cannot even save himself: "All right. Let it happen. I'll go ahead and die" (263, *257*).

So "sick" is Ezra for the home he recalls as happy and loving—so homesick, that is, "for a home he never [really] had"[13]—that he is able to channel whatever energy and selfhood he does possess only into yet another home, the Homesick Restaurant. It originally belonged to Mrs. Scarlatti, a kind of surrogate mother so deeply attuned to him that she called him "my boy" (94, *93*) while he, the nearest thing to next of kin for her, was left to make her funeral arrangements. In contrast to Pearl, who (like Cody) demands complete control, Mrs. Scarlatti permits a more give-and-take relationship with Ezra. They can even disagree: with Mrs. Scarlatti dying in the hospital, Ezra, her sole heir and business partner, redesigns the interior of their restaurant, knocking down walls to suit his own personal vision. Mrs. Scarlatti, in a brief period of remission, discovers the truth; but after her initial sense of horror and betrayal, the relationship readjusts and continues.[14] It is an important experience for Ezra, who begins to make radical changes in personnel and menus—but who yet cannot leave the "safe" environment of the homelike restaurant to which he has dedicated his life: the meals simply become more homey (including "consoling" pot roast [139, *136*] and gizzard soup "made with love" [132, *130*]), the decor becomes increasingly domestic, and the businesslike waiters are replaced by "cheery, motherly

UNDERSTANDING ANNE TYLER

waitresses" (124, *122*). Imprisoned in one form of home or another,[15] Ezra seems doomed to remain forever in his present situation, repetitively insisting upon holding "real family dinners" that the family does not want.

Both Cody the "bad" dark son and Ezra the "good" blond son seem locked in their mindsets, and at first glance there would seem to be no help for them. As Jenny muses on the brink of her breakdown, "Was this what it came to—that you never could escape? That certain things were doomed to continue, generation after generation?" (214, *209*). The answer is no, as her subsequent mental collapse and concomitant reappraisal of her mother reveals. We are not "doomed" to do anything by virtue of either upbringing or genes; but it is likewise untrue either that "What happens, happens" (176, *172*)—an attitude implying that life is beyond either control or meaning—or that "We make our own luck" (200, *196*)—one that implies our total control. The answer is somewhere in between. As Mary Ellis Gibson has observed, "Tyler never quite becomes either a fatalist or a nihilist, though both attitudes seem possible given the human situation as she sees it."[16] Tyler is arguing, as she has argued in most of her earlier novels, that change and adversity are inevitable, and that one must endure them; or as Mrs. Scarlatti phrases matters, "Life is a continual shoring up" (101, *99*). If one's capacity for "shoring up" is not part of one's inherited temperament or childhood training, then one can actively cultivate it.

DINNER AT THE HOMESICK RESTAURANT

Again, Jenny seems to be Tyler's spokesperson. She can look with bemusement at her "old" self, the one that resembled a concentration camp victim in an old photograph, or that inexplicably loved the movie *A Taste of Honey*, without feeling that there is some debilitating loss of identity or stability involved. She simply is "a different person" (210, *206*) at different stages of her life; and as an adult she can—and must—put into clearer and more compassionate perspective the negative experiences of that earlier self:

"It's whether you add up the list or not," Jenny said. "I mean, if you catalogue grudges, anything looks bad. And Cody certainly catalogues; he's running his life with his catalogues. But after all, I told him, we made it, didn't we? We did grow up. Why, the three of us turned out fine, just fine!" (204, *200*)

Jenny's epiphany holds out the possibility of hope for her siblings. Ezra, passive though he may be, responds immediately to the justice of Jenny's statement: "'It's true,' said Ezra, his forehead smoothing" (204, *200*). And though he continues his practice of arranging family dinners, he does so not out of his earlier compulsion, but out of a sincere desire to express his love for his family and to urge them to express it as well. He even invites the long-estranged Beck Tull to the post-funeral dinner in a dramatic example of refusing to continue clinging to the "catalogue" of ill will. It does not matter that Beck mistakes the salad boys for his own grandchildren or that he assumes incorrectly that Becky was named after him. What matters is that Cody, brought face to face with his father for the first time in decades, suddenly realizes that a major unconscious factor in his drive for success was his desire to impress his father ("Was this all he had been striving for—this one brief moment of respect flitting across his father's face?" [298, *291*]) and that Beck had abandoned his family not as a punishment for an unknown mistake on Cody's part but as a response to his inability to deal with "the grayness; grayness of things; half-right-and-half-wrongness of things" (308, *301*). However much she may empathize with Beck Tull's dismay,[17] Tyler nevertheless argues that everyone—the Tulls, the bereaved truck driver, the divorced father seeking old girlfriends, Liddie's distraught mother, endlessly driving the Beltway in search of juvenile hitchhikers—must deal with that grayness, must develop some strategy of endurance.

And for the first time in her writings, Tyler argues that three elements which often seemed problematic in the pursuit of that strategy—outsiders, genetics, and time itself—could actually contribute positively to the process. For example, Ezra's interaction with a non-family member, Mrs. Scarlatti, ultimately fostered the evolution of "his own adult identity," an evolution requiring the symbolic demolition of his attachment to both his real and surrogate mothers.[18] More subtly, young Luke shows the potential benefit of genetics in the process: he has his Uncle Ezra's walk as well as his yellow hair and gray eyes; but he is like his father Cody in his tone of voice and the way he moves his shoulders, and from a distance he could be mistaken for his Grandfather Beck. Physical characteristics thus are inherited, and so are certain aspects of temperament, for Luke also has Ezra's love of music. But far more to the point, the whole is far greater than the sum of the parts: though Luke is a little like all the other men in his family, he is quite unlike them in his clear vision and fundamental good sense. He realizes that his father clings to self-destructive, distortive memories, and urges him, forthrightly, to change: "What are you, crazy? How come you go on hanging *on* to these things, year after year after year?" (261, 255). Granted, Tyler is not so ingenuous as to suggest that the process is invariably ameliorative across generations; Jenny's daughter, after all, likewise develops eating disorders, whether due to parental example or inherited temperament. But Tyler at least holds out the hope that future generations could, like Luke, be able to break the cycles of ill will, guilt, and abuse. And Tyler also suggests that the breaking can occur in one's own lifetime if one is receptive to the clearer perspective, compassion, and maturity that so often come with the passage of time. Both Jenny and Ezra reach this stage in middle age, and Tyler leaves the reader with the impression that Cody, having met the dreaded Beck after thirty-five years of bitter estrangement, may be "somewhat liberated" by the encounter.[19] Thus, even though Tyler's vision in *Dinner at the Homesick Restaurant* is rather dark—it is difficult, after all, not to feel that the Tull children are unusually fortunate in their capacity to grow beyond the debilitating effects of their "homesickness"—it is hardly the case that the novel offers a "deterministic" world view.[20] Without resorting to a "feel good" happy ending, Tyler holds out the possibility that eventually the Tull family, present and future, will come to recognize that it really is a *"beautiful green little planet"* (284, 277) after all.

Notes

1. Quoted in Sarah English, "Anne Tyler," in *The Dictionary of Literary Biography Yearbook: 1982* (Detroit: Gale Research, 1983): 194.

2. Doris Betts notes that "homesick" conveys "Tyler's usual paradox: sick FOR home, sick OF home" ("The Fiction of Anne Tyler," *Southern Quarterly* 21 [Summer 1983]: 35). Mary F. Robertson argues that "homesick" is "a pun": "if too much ingrown, or if conceived of as the place of a golden age," then a home "is sick" ("Anne Tyler: Medusa Points and Contact Points," in Catherine Rainwater and William J. Scheick, eds., *Contemporary American Women Writers: Narrative Strategies* [Lexington: UP of Kentucky, 1985]: 134).

3. R. Z. Sheppard, "Eat and Run," *Time* 119 (5 April 1982): 77.

4. Mary Ellis Gibson, "Family as Fate: The Novels of Anne Tyler," *Southern Literary Journal* 16 (Fall 1983): 51.

5. In one of the most negative reviews of *Dinner at the Homesick Restaurant*, James Wolcott argues that the novel "is hobbled from

page one on by its rickety plot structure. . . . Deathbed retrospectives have been worked to the nub in fiction, and Tyler doesn't come up with any spiffy ways to soup up and customize her time machine. She simply creaks through her characters' pasts, scooping up mementos and scattering them across the table like a palmful of seashells" ("Strange New World," *Esquire* 97 [April 1982]: 124). For an interesting, if sometimes strained, study of the parallels between *Dinner* and Faulkner's *As I Lay Dying,* see Mary J. Elkins, "*Dinner at the Homesick Restaurant:* Anne Tyler and the Faulkner Connection," *Atlantis* 10 (Spring 1985): 93–105.

6. Anne G. Jones, "Home at Last, and Homesick Again: The Ten Novels of Anne Tyler," *The Hollins Critic* 23 (April 1986): 10. Writes Doris Betts, herself a novelist, "Some story writers who take up novels cannot break the habit of producing each chapter like a mini-story, one bead on a string of beads. Last month, by accident, I met Anne Tyler's mother, Phyllis, who told me every titled chapter in *Homesick Restaurant* had been designed so it could be published as a separate story. I had not noticed" (36).

7. English 192.

8. John Updike, "On Such a Beautiful Green Little Planet," *The New Yorker* 58 (5 April 1982): 195.

9. Anne G. Jones argues that at "crucial moments," Cody "will protect Ezra—from getting lost in a crowd, from a woman who doesn't appreciate him—so deeply connected are Cody's envy and his love" (11). Mary F. Robertson theorizes that "through Ruth, Cody is able in part to incorporate that lost part of himself—the brother whom he so wished to be like" (131–32). In contrast, Vivian Gornick does not detect the love at the center of the Tulls' relationships: "Unable to hate his mother openly, Cody displaces this hatred onto soft, dreamy Ezra" ("Anne Tyler's Arrested Development," *The Village Voice* 27 [30 March 1982]: 41).

10. Elkins 102.

11. "I hope you won't think I'm being facetious when I say that my earliest and perhaps strongest literary influence was a children's

picture book called *The Little House* by Virginia Lee Burton. I still read it" (quoted in Laurie L. Brown, "Interviews with Seven Contemporary Writers," *Southern Quarterly* 21 [Summer 1983]: 11).

12. Robertson 131.

13. Elkins 100.

14. Writes Anne G. Jones, "for Ezra to grow, to move into competence and a separate self, would mean the loss of his mother's love. It's a plot he acts out clearly with Mrs. Scarlatti. When he designs her restaurant in his own vision of a good fit between feeder and fed, Ezra loses her love" (11). This does not seem to be the case for, as Mary F. Robertson observes, Ezra does not change the restaurant back to the way it was, and Mrs. Scarlatti does not change her mind about leaving it to him (130).

15. Wolcott describes the Homesick Restaurant as "really a boarded-up prison—a roomy crypt" (124). Though this is the case for a while, Ezra by the end of the novel seems to be breaking free of his compulsion to lock himself away in his home and his home-like restaurant.

16. Gibson 57.

17. Doris Betts argues that "this runaway father seems to summarize for Tyler what she considers semi-heroic. Beck Tull admires but cannot be like those who can endure 'the grayness of things, the half-right and half-wrongness of things,' the stay-at-homes who cope." Betts estimates that "40 percent of [Tyler's] heart" is always "running away" from the idea of compromise and endurance, "and fleeing for dear life with the non-conformists" like Beck. She surmises further that Tyler "must evidently keep working through her long stay-and-go conflict over and over, book after book" (35–36).

18. Robertson stresses the importance of outsiders in breaking down the strangle-hold of family influence: "The Tull family is finally like this restaurant itself: the shell of the original still stands, but the interior has been demolished and refashioned through the beneficial agency of significant outsiders" (134).

19. Robertson 134.

20. Elkins maintains that Tyler's is a "deterministic world" (98), while Updike feels that the novel depicts "the tragedy of closeness": "familial limitations . . . work upon us like Greek fates and condemn us to lives of surrender and secret fury" (194). Though Tyler would seem to believe that this can and does happen, she still feels just as strongly that it can be dealt with constructively. There is nothing in the Tyler canon to place her within the Naturalistic school of thought.

CHAPTER NINE

The Accidental Tourist

Anne Tyler's tenth novel, *The Accidental Tourist* (1985), is very much of a piece with her earlier efforts. Peter S. Prescott of *Newsweek* observes dryly that the "markings" on it as a Tyler novel are "as distinctive as those on a Japanese print, or on the back of a silver spoon. The first stands for 'Baltimore.' The next reads 'delicate balance of comedy and pathos.' The third: 'tensions of domesticity.' The last: 'temptations of order and chaos.'"[1] Prescott's statement is accurate only as far as it goes; for if one could reduce *The Accidental Tourist* to a formula, one could not explain why reading it is such a satisfying experience, or why it garnered more popular and critical acclaim than even *Dinner at the Homesick Restaurant*. Brigitte Weeks spoke for many in terming it, "quite simply, her best novel yet. [Tyler's] place in American fiction is now secure."[2] The source of its impact is not the familiarity of its features, however comforting they may be to Tyler devotees; rather, the strong suit of *The Accidental Tourist* is the refinement of Tyler's ideas and, concomitantly, the skill and originality in-

volved in their presentation. Avoiding the technical vir-
tuosity that had proved to be a sometimes distracting
element in novels like *Celestial Navigation* and *Earthly
Possessions,* Tyler offers an atypically straightforward,
chronological narrative, one interwoven with brief
flashbacks and dreams, and presented from the point
of view of just one character. The stripped-down format
imparts great intensity to her psychological portrait of
Macon Leary, while enabling—indeed, compelling—her
to avoid the seemingly too-easy resolutions that, in the
minds of some readers, had marred novels like *Searching
for Caleb* and *Morgan's Passing.*

Not everyone can effect a psychologically satisfying
compromise to knotty questions of identity, love, and
work by running away to join a traveling entertainment
troupe, that almost fairy tale solution to very real, adult
problems; nor can everyone, like Charlotte Emory, simply return to an unsatisfying existence, bolstered by a
chipper faith in the efficacy of "Keep on Truckin'." The
resolutions of those earlier novels confirmed that they
were, at heart, essentially allegories, with characters
(such as Daniel and Caleb Peck) baldly representing
personality types, spiritual states, or possible life
choices. In *The Accidental Tourist,* although Tyler does
to a certain degree retain an allegorical dimension, pos-
iting Macon as a kind of reluctant Everyman traveling
along life's difficult road—hence the punning surname,
"Leary," and the anonymity of the guidebooks ("No
author's name, just a logo" [11, *12*])[3]—she has essen-

tially abandoned this venerable fictional mode in favor of humor-tinged realism, an approach that can offer only a guardedly hopeful resolution in an essentially "open" ending.[4] As he works his way to the painful realization that compromise is rarely feasible in this complex world, that the most one can hope for is to "choose what to lose" (301, *310*), Macon is depicted first "crumbling" (137, *144*), then regrouping with the help of outside agents and pressures, and ultimately emerging as a man as happy as it is possible for him to be. Macon Leary ends up, indeed, as something quite rare in post-World War II fiction: a hero of sorts.

One hardly would expect this at the opening of *The Accidental Tourist*. Always a rather timid man, Macon becomes emphatically "leery" of life as the result of the senseless murder of his son Ethan and his subsequent separation from his wife Sarah. Essentially he barricades himself in his Baltimore home, venturing out to buy groceries only on Tuesdays, "when the supermarket was least crowded with other human beings" (54, *56*). Less obvious is the fact that he muffles himself increasingly in neurotic routines and what he charitably terms "system" (8, *9*): obsessed with the ideas of sanitation and the conservation of energy, he uses the dishwasher sparingly, letting dirty crockery pile up in his bleach-disinfected sink; he disconnects the clothes dryer, thereby saving on both electricity and kitty litter as his cat Helen uses the exhaust tube as her personal pet door; he does his laundry as he showers, stomping his clothes with his feet and letting them dry in the bathroom overnight. Matters worsen, as his behavior slips from eccentric to neurotic to compulsive. Macon begins to wear sweat suits in lieu of both daytime clothes and pajamas, and sets up his coffee-maker and popcorn popper by his bed to save all those steps to the kitchen every morning. Extra walking is, after all, wasteful—and it also is increasingly difficult, as Macon sinks ever more deeply into acute depression. He even begins to sleep in sewn-together sheets, ostensibly to spare himself the rigors of tucking them in, but in fact to cut himself off from the world even more completely. The "Macon Leary Body Bag" (10, *11*), its name and concept drawn from the "body bags" used to transport American servicemen killed in Vietnam, is the ideal symbol of the psychic death Macon is undergoing due to the tragedies in his life.

His spirit, however, is not entirely gone: he knows that what he is doing is evasive and, ironically, counter-productive. The body bags, far from saving time and energy, only yield "quite a lot of sheets" for the washing machine (10, *11*); the sweat suits, instead of sparing Macon the stress of making decisions about what to wear, only create more problems by failing to dry over-night; further, the sweat suits are enervating in their very comfort, as Macon suddenly realizes: "What a mistake! He felt like a fool. He'd come within an inch, within a hairsbreadth of turning into one of those pa-thetic creatures you see on the loose from time to time—

unwashed, unshaven, shapeless, talking to themselves, padding along in their institutional garb" (56, *58*). But realizing there is a problem is one thing, while solving it is another; and so, unable to stop what he is doing ("there was such a danger in falling behind with your system" [15, *16*]), Macon persists in what even he knows is "carrying things too far" (10, *11*). Finally, he breaks his leg while falling over a laundry basket strapped to a skateboard, and thus is forced to regress even further, to move back into the comfortingly familiar, sealed household of his childhood. Surrounded by sister Rose and brothers Porter and Charles, those middle-aged "boys" (308, *317*), Macon stands only to compound his problems in the act of evading them.

Firmly ensconced in their grandparents' home where they grew up, the Leary children are safe in an orderly world where groceries are alphabetized esoterically (elbow macaroni goes under *E*, not *M* [macaroni], *N* [noodles], or *P* [pasta] [88, *92*]), where *"conservative"* (74, *77*) baked potatoes with American paprika are *de rigueur*, and where the telephone, that traditional Tyler symbol of tenuous contact with the frightening outside world, rings ignored day after day. Looking unsettlingly like themselves in their childhood portrait, the Learys are Peckish in their refusal to use "ballpoint pens or electric typewriters or automatic transmissions" (132, *138*) and secure in their devotion to "morning" and "evening" coffee (143, *149*) served in mugs inscribed "CENTURY OF PROGRESS 1933" (122, *127–28*). They are in fact rather extreme even for eccentrics, and several critics, including the usually laudatory John Updike, seem put off by their antics.[5] But as Rose Leary herself observes, "We're the most conventional people I know" (122, *127*). When conventionality, "normalcy," is taken to extremes, it becomes grotesque, unconventional, abnormal.[6] Though Tyler has many times argued that "good" things, including family togetherness, can be counterproductive under certain circumstances, never before has she exposed so vigorously the downside of even the virtual rallying cry of her earlier novels, the need for endurance.

Goodness knows the Leary children have endured. They have managed to make it to middle age with nary a ripple in the placid surfaces of their lives, surviving brief forays into such dark waters as sex ("it's rather messy" [238, *249*]) and unfamiliar Baltimore neighborhoods, where thanks to their "geographic dyslexia" (111, *116*) they become lost even on the way to the hardware store. Nonetheless, their lives are encircled by perils including, ironically, many of their own making. What with the ant poison stored alphabetically next to the allspice and the potentially lethal Thanksgiving turkey slow-cooked overnight to conserve energy, the Learys endanger themselves in the very act of creating an orderly, sealed environment. As is signified by the name of their impossibly complicated family card game, "Vaccination," the Learys feel that they have created a world inoculated against pain and tribulation. It is, unfortunately, a world which no one else can enter. The rules are known only to them.

Macon grew up in that world, and he feels safe there. Indeed, he even wonders whether he had subconsciously engineered his broken leg so that he could return there. For a time he relishes the regression, gloating like a child that his estranged wife, boss, and neighbors have no idea where he is, and enjoying the sensation of his cast sealing him away from everything, including his own troubled self: "Sometimes he wished he could stay in his cast forever. In fact, he wished it covered him from head to foot" (120, 125). He easily could spend the rest of an increasingly reclusive life in the enervating confines of the Leary home, could technically "endure" the loss of Ethan and Sarah. But despite his initial contentedness and his seeming oneness with his siblings, Macon is different enough from them not to remain in his childhood environment indefinitely. Eventually he will venture out again; but this slow process—one that goes against Macon's temperament, upbringing, and experience-based fears—must be facilitated by a series of events and agents drawing out his own personal resiliency.

Ironically, the first of these agents is his broken leg. Though its cast is the physical embodiment of what Sarah regards as his primary problem—"you're ossified. You're encased. You're like something in a capsule. You're a dried-up kernel of a man that nothing real penetrates" (136, 142)—it also is the means by which

THE ACCIDENTAL TOURIST

Macon acquires a broader perspective on life. Thanks to his disability, Macon must walk slowly and carefully, as a result of which he "saw much more than he would have otherwise" (105, *109*). For example, though he had been eating at the Old Bay Restaurant for many years—as, indeed, had his grandfather and great-grandfather before him—he "hadn't even noticed" the marble steps at its entrance until he was forced to maneuver them on crutches (125, *130*). Long after his cast is removed the improved perception continues, as he discovers an incomprehensible object in a Winnipeg hotel room that he'd never noticed during two previous stays there. Like the kidnapping in *Earthly Possessions*, the broken leg is the unlikely agent of improved vision, not just for restaurant steps and Canadian light fixtures, but more importantly for life choices and self-image. But before Macon can be receptive to the lessons to be learned from the broken leg, he must deal with a series of human agents who clarify the significance of what he is seeing.

One of these agents is his dead son, Ethan—or, more precisely, the Ethan of memory and dream. Though he is a questionable device in the opinions of many commentators,[7] he actually is as effective as Janie Rose Pike in *The Tin Can Tree* in serving as a catalyst for both action and evaluation. The victim of a senseless execution-style slaying during a robbery at a fast-food restaurant a year before the story opens, young Ethan continues to bring forth many of Macon's deepest concerns. The product of a marriage based on a fundamental fraudulence—teen-aged Macon had actively cultivated a facade of coolness and withdrawal in his ploy to win Sarah Sidey, and had somehow become what he affected—Ethan's conception had generated guilt in Macon, whose ever-logical mind had explained seven years' failure to conceive as indicative of his and Sarah's "essential incompatibility" (130, *136*). But little Ethan also had compounded Macon's innate terror of the world: insulating the boy's bedroom with "jokey stickers" from Wacky Packs and forcing him to learn to swing a bat at age six, Macon felt he was protecting his son from "every eventuality" (16, *17*)—every one, that is, except for an encounter with a trigger-happy teen thug at a Burger Bonanza. As with most Tyler characters, Macon tries frantically to blame someone for the tragedy—"blame even (hell, yes) Ethan" himself (17, *19*). But blame implies the possibility of responsible, foresightful action in a logical, cause-and-effect world; and what Macon had never realized until his son's death is that the world is largely an "evil" one, where horrible things truly do happen to good, innocent people for no discernible reason. This realization incapacitates Sarah, who is not "sure I could live in this kind of a world anymore" (134, *140*):

"Macon," she said, "ever since Ethan died I've had to admit that people are basically bad. Evil, Macon. So evil they would take a twelve-year-old boy and shoot him through the skull for no reason. I read a paper now and I despair; I've given up watching the news on TV. There's so much wickedness, children setting other children on fire and grown men throwing babies out second-story windows, rape and torture and terrorism, old people beaten and robbed, men in our very own government willing to blow up the world, indifference and greed and instant anger on every street corner." (133, 139–40)[8]

This realization has also, of course, largely incapacitated Macon, who has built a career out of writing guidebooks for people who, like him, are terrified of the world.

The motif of accidental tourism is, as Adam Mars-Jones avers, "undoubtedly hammered home,"[9] but it still is effective in conveying Tyler's ideas. Macon truly hates to travel, yet he does it for a living. He could of course return to work at the Leary family's factory, an inherited firm that manufactures the cork-lined bottle caps that were essentially obsolete from the moment pop-top aluminum cans came on the market in the 1960s. It would be a safe, if dated and rather pointless, occupation. But by being the globetrotting compiler of guidebooks, Macon is illustrating his fundamental differentness from the other Learys (he had "wasted away with boredom" at the factory [77, 79]), plus the perverseness of this illogical world—one so illogical that Julian Edge and Rose Leary fall in love[10]—and, perhaps most important, the appropriateness of travel as the emblem of man's passage through life. Though it is hardly an original concept (witness John Bunyan's seven-teenth-century *Pilgrim's Progress*), it has been given a timely look and a timely relevance in *The Accidental Tourist*. With his free-floating anxiety conveniently dis-placed into a terror of unknown baggage handlers and *"foreign laundries"* (24, 25), Macon formulates a series of strategies for minimalizing contact with these entities: *"Bring only what fits in a carry-on bag"*; *"Add several travel-size packets of detergent"*; *"Always bring a book, as protection against strangers"* (24, 30, 25, 31).[11] And his system of rules works: as fellow passenger Lucas Loomis an-nounces with glee, "Times I've flown clear to Oregon and hardly knew I'd left Baltimore" (243, 253). The uni-formly passport-size guidebooks would appear thus to be impervious shields against the foreignness, the un-known, the "evil" of the world; but in fact they speak to the centrality of change while brushing past the be-nignity and excitement that co-exist with its terrors.

As Macon's boss Julian points out, "Things are changing every minute, Macon. Change! It's what keeps us in the black" (87, 90). Each volume must be constantly updated as hotels and restaurants fall into the hands of new, alien managers (or old managers with new, alien ideas), and Macon thus is trapped in an end-less cycle of revisiting cities and revising books. He is, in effect, building a career on the fact of change without even realizing it. Further, a central aspect of that change is the steady, insidious absorption of the unknown into the familiar. His guidebooks direct Yankee tourists to

Taco Bells in Mexico City and to restaurants in Rome that serve Chef Boyardee ravioli—Mexican and Italian foods that have been so absorbed into the American consciousness that they have come to be regarded as quintessentially American. Even pita bread can be purchased in Stockholm: Macon "wasn't sure how it had happened, but lately pita had grown to seem as American as hot dogs" (11, *13*). Not until he can understand and accept this phenomenon, not until he can comprehend that change is not necessarily debilitating, can Macon be responsive to San Francisco as a kind of "Emerald City" (243, *254*)—and to the death of Ethan and the departure of Sarah as changes that will leave him, like his broken leg, stronger than ever.

That realization is, however, a long time coming. For much of the novel he continues to be an "accidental" tourist, as opposed to a "reluctant" one (Julian's original title for the guidebook series [85, *89*]). Many of the things that occur during Macon's travels through life are indeed "accidents" in the usual, negative sense of the word, including the senseless death of Ethan and the equally meaningless death of Dominick Saddler in a car wreck. But "accidents" are not necessarily bad. Macon has no intention of taking his dog Edward to the Meow-Bow, but having been turned away from his usual vet and with a plane departure imminent, Macon simply goes to the first kennel he sees. Utter serendipity. Or is it? Much as Macon feels that, on some level, the breaking of his leg was no accident, it is difficult not to suspect that the meeting with Muriel Pritchett was part of a larger plan. Some religions and certain fields of psychology maintain, after all, that there is no such thing as an accident, good or bad, while physicists are currently exploring the "science of chaos"—one which argues that chaos does not in fact exist. Though, as noted in the previous chapter, Tyler is neither a fatalist nor a nihilist, and though she goes to great lengths never to speak of a Judeo-Christian God (except to satirize ministers), Tyler does seem to feel that there is a pattern and purpose underlying what happens to people—or, barring that, that people have the capacity to rationalize that this is the case in order to render life's vicissitudes tolerable. Given this situation, it was inevitable that Macon—essentially a survivor, and different enough from his siblings to be married for twenty years—would find Muriel, or someone very much like her: an agent able to put matters into perspective for him while articulating truths that should have been self-evident.

Hence the significance of the fact that it is his dog Edward who is responsible for bringing them together. As is signified by his desire to see hotel rooms supplied with "optional small animals" (150, *157*), Macon realizes well that there is a close spiritual and emotional kinship between people and their domestic pets; and though Tyler has been praised effusively for her depiction of Edward, what matters more than his charm is his capacity to embody and express the psychological needs of his owner.[12] Macon himself is too rigid and "muffled" (135, *142*) to articulate the rage, confusion, and frustration he feels over the tragedies in his life, so it is the dog who effectively responds on his behalf: "Could a dog have a nervous breakdown?" (27). Evidently so, as he urinates excessively as a would-be "adjustment to change" (61, *62*), pursues hapless bikers, and, in general, "hates the whole world" (117, *123*). Macon hates it as well, although as a man and an ultra-conservative Leary he cannot permit himself to express this. His psychological crippling is reflected in his physical disability, with Edward "matching Macon's gait so perfectly that he looked crippled himself" (119, *124*). And when Edward attacks Macon, it symbolizes the self-destructiveness underlying his emotional state. But even that incident is not enough to compel him to seek professional help for the dog: he refuses to take action against Edward, not only because he was Ethan's pet, and hence one of the last living links to his dead son, but also because Edward is the only outlet he possesses for his own psychological distress.

Yet at some point that distress must be acknowledged and controlled. Enter Muriel the dog-trainer, whose own life—an unhappy early marriage, borderline poverty, a seriously ill son, uncomprehending parents—has been in its way as difficult as his: as her Caesarean incision suggests, *"I'm scarred, too. We're all scarred. You are not the only one"* (191, *201*). But Muriel has several distinct advantages over Macon. For one thing, she can communicate. Using a system of taps, clucks, and finger signals, Muriel is able to tame Edward in a process that is as slow, and occasionally as seemingly hopeless, as the taming of Macon's fear and anger. Though "communicate" is Macon's "least favorite word" (131, 137)—indeed, a year after the fact he had never actually said that his son was dead, while he sabotages meaningful dialogue by perpetually correcting other people's pronunciation and word choice—he learns through Muriel that he must communicate if he is to survive. Eventually, Macon finds himself talking frequently to Muriel about Ethan. "It felt good to say his name out loud" (219, 229).

Muriel also articulates for Macon what he could not accept in his guilt-ridden conviction that he had failed to protect Ethan: "You can take protection too far" (93, 97). Armed with tiny packets of detergent and always wearing a gray suit in the event of *"sudden funerals"* (24)—on a business trip?—Macon is perpetually ready for emergencies that never emerge. He does not realize the wisdom of Muriel's statement until a flight across Canada, when he tries to console a fellow passenger with a glass of his ever-ready, carry-on sherry. He literally had never opened his travel flask "because he'd gone on saving it for some occasion even worse than whatever the current one was, something that never quite arrived. Like his other emergency supplies . . . this flask was being hoarded for the *real* emergency. In fact, its metal lid had grown rusty inside" (285, 295). One can never be prepared for every tragedy, such as the murder of Ethan—but one can easily be incapacitated by over-preparing for tragedies that never happen.

And although tragedies and emergencies rarely occur, those which do occur can usually be handled—and often with help from strangers. This too is an important lesson offered by Muriel, who trains Macon as much as she trains the anthropomorphic Edward. At times this animal-handler's ability to handle things renders her something of a caricature. She recalls how once, with a broken arm, she fought off a potentially lethal attack by a Doberman by asserting "Absolutely not" (109, *114*). She foils a would-be mugger by slamming him with her purse and ordering him to "get on home this instant or you'll be sorry you were ever born": ". . . why, Muriel hadn't even seemed surprised. She might have strolled down that street expecting a neighbor here, a stray dog there, a holdup just beyond—all equally part of life. [Macon] felt awed by her" (269, *279–80*). Muriel is more believable, and hence more effective, in her visit to France. Though she has been warned by Macon that "'Paris is terrible. Everybody's impolite'" (99, *104*), she has no trouble navigating the unfamiliar streets, makes excellent thrift-shop deals despite knowing nothing about French money, and finds the notorious Parisian waiters unfailingly helpful. Though Macon tries to restore his image of France by declaring her experiences atypical ("That was a rare exception" [327, *338*]), even Macon—incapacitated by a trick back as earlier he had been by a broken leg—must come to admit that one can depend on the good graces of others to help one handle life's difficulties. That his lifelong negative impression of the French could have been totally unfounded forces him to re-evaluate his sense of the world at large as overwhelming. True, Macon cannot, and will not, deny that the world has some evil elements, but he at least allows himself to admit that, as with Muriel's seemingly treacherous Singleton Street neighborhood, there is a comforting sense of community underlying even the least promising situations. Macon finds it " 'heartening' " that "most human beings do try. How they try to be as responsible and kind as they can manage" despite all (338, 350).

All this is not to say that the trip through life is necessarily pleasant or easy. Bringing a child into the world does not mean he won't be murdered in a Burger Bonanza, nor are there any guarantees that he will even be healthy. Muriel's son Alexander, a sickly child believed to be allergic to air, is a living emblem of the dangers of the outside world: "Whenever he's outside a long time he gets these bumps on any uncovered parts of his body" (185, 195). But most of Alexander's problems can be dealt with: his real ailments can be treated with medication, his self-image can be enhanced with something as simple as comfortable boys' clothing from a Western shop, and his psychosomatic disorders—such as being allergic to milk enzymes in the morning but not in the afternoon—can be resolved with common sense and direct experience. If Alexander will never be the brightest or the strongest boy in his class, he will at least be happy.

Ultimately that is the attitude Macon acquires by the end of the novel. Much to his astonishment, he begins to perceive that he is, after all, a "merry, tolerant person" (287, *298*), one who can buffet life's inevitable jolts as readily as he survives repeated bumps from kneecap-high Canadian kindergarteners: "No harm done" (288, *298*). His good-natured, patient attentions to the elderly Mrs. Bunn, a white-knuckled fellow passenger on the plane to Edmonton, is thus not a shortcoming in the novel or an inconsistency in the depiction of Macon.[13] Rather, it is the confirmation of his abandonment of his cocoon of isolationism, of a mindset which had been destructive to Macon in its insistence on the need for order, consistency, and safety. Even love and marriage are re-evaluated: "he began to believe that people could, in fact, be used up—could use each other up, could be of no further help to each other and maybe even do harm to each other. He began to think that who you are when you're with somebody may matter more than whether you love her" (307, *317*). And so he abandons the comfortingly familiar Sarah in his Paris hotel room. And he leaves the symbol of his terror of change and the alien world, his carry-on bag of emergency items, on a Paris curb—for, "lightweight though it was, it twisted his back out of line" (341, 353). And he embraces the new and the different, Muriel Pritchett.[14]

Some critics have faulted *The Accidental Tourist* for being predictable, soap operatic, and sentimental,[15] and to a certain extent it is all of these. But it also is more honest and realistic than anything Tyler has yet written and, in many ways, more wise. It confirms the tragi-comic nature of the world without suggesting that a happy compromise is somehow possible to enable one to deal with it. That one must "choose what to lose" implies inevitable loss. No matter what Macon does, either Sarah or Muriel will be hurt. (In contrast, Morgan Gower had it easy in choosing Emily, secure in the knowledge that his feisty, independently wealthy wife would do just fine without him.) But choosing what to lose also confirms the efficacy of choice, and Macon heroically chooses to pursue "the real adventure" (342, 354), pain and all.

Notes

1. Peter S. Prescott, "Watching Life Go By," *Newsweek* 106 (9 September 1985): 92.

2. Brigitte Weeks, [rev. of *The Accidental Tourist*], *Ms.* 14 (November 1985): 28. Jonathan Yardley was even more emphatic: "Words fail me: one cannot reasonably expect fiction to be much better than this" ("Anne Tyler's Family Circles," *Washington Post Book World* [25

THE ACCIDENTAL TOURIST

August 1985]: 3). *The Accidental Tourist* enjoyed a high degree of public exposure. It had a first printing of 75,000 copies, was a Book of the Month Club main selection, and was made into a Warner Brothers motion picture starring William Hurt [Macon], Kathleen Turner [Sarah], and Geena Davis, who won an Academy Award for Best Supporting Actress in the role of Muriel.

3. Weeks aptly describes Macon as an Everyman figure (28). Anne R. Zahlan points out that Macon is "Leary of life, as his name suggests" ("Anne Tyler," in Joseph M. Flora and Robert Bain, eds., *Fifty Southern Writers After 1900: A Bio-Bibliographical Sourcebook* [Westport, Connecticut: Greenwood Press, 1987]: 499).

4. Joseph Mathewson comments on the fundamental hopefulness of Tyler's world view: "These days, the few good writers who also dare to be hopeful provide themselves with the safety net of an ultimate worldly cynicism (like John Irving). Miss Tyler does her act without the net" ("Taking the Anne Tyler Tour," *Horizon* 28 [September 1985]: 14). Peter S. Prescott notes that Tyler goes no further than to indicate that Macon makes a difficult choice: "Like most novelists—think of Henry James, sending Isabel Archer back to her husband—Tyler spares us the sight of what happens next" (92).

5. Updike feels that "some of the Learys' behavior seems unlikely even for reclusive and order-obsessed eccentrics" ("Leaving Home," *The New Yorker* 61 [28 October 1985]: 107). Michiko Kakutani argues that "the Learys are so predictable in their willful fuddy-duddiness that Miss Tyler's portrait seems at first to verge on caricature . . . In the past, her affection for her characters, her endless tolerance for their failings, has hovered on the edge of sentimentality, but in 'The Accidental Tourist' she simply draws upon this sympathy, using it to show us the inner workings of her people's psyches and to burnish the entire novel with the luster of acceptance" ([rev. of *The Accidental Tourist*], *The New York Times* [28 August 1985], Sec. C: 21).

6. Prescott argues that the situation inverts the customary Tyler approach: "In 'Morgan's Passing' and 'Dinner at the Homesick Restaurant,' eccentric or extravagant characters dream of a more orderly

life. In 'The Accidental Tourist,' Tyler reverses her perspective: the orderly life, taken to an extreme, becomes a deadening cocoon" (92).

7. Larry McMurtry feels that, "despite an effort now and then to bring him into the book in a vignette or a nightmare, Ethan remains mostly a premise, and one not advanced very confidently by the author" ("Life Is a Foreign Country," *New York Times Book Review* [8 September 1985]: 36).

8. *The Accidental Tourist* is yet another Tyler novel striking for its echoes of Transcendental thought. Sarah's dismay over reports in the media of human cruelty calls to mind Henry David Thoreau's statement that "if we read of one man robbed, or murdered, or killed by accident, or one house burned, or one vessel wrecked, or one steamboat blown up, or one cow run over on the Western Railroad, or one mad dog killed, or one lot of grasshoppers in the winter,—we never need read of another. One is enough." In the same chapter of *Walden*, he remarks that "We do not ride on the railroad; it rides upon us"—a statement reminiscent of Julian's sensation that Rose could not help but return to her old neighborhood to chauffeur her elderly neighbors: "she turned and stared, and I got the funniest feeling, like the car was driving *her*" (308, *318*). Even Thoreau's observation that "We are determined to be starved before we are hungry. Men say that a stitch in time saves nine, and so they take a thousand stitches to-day to save nine to-morrow" conveys perfectly Macon's unwitting creation of more work for himself in his determination to conserve labor. (See the chapter entitled "What I Lived For" in Henry David Thoreau, *Walden* [1854].) Although Thoreau seeks to expose the hypocrisy and wastefulness of a rapidly industrializing nineteenth-century America while Tyler is exploring the psychological ramifications of stress and neurosis in the twentieth, *Walden* is an illuminating book to read in conjunction with *The Accidental Tourist* and most of Tyler's other novels.

9. Adam Mars-Jones, "Despairs of a time-and-motion man," *[London] Times Literary Supplement* (4 October 1985): 1096.

10. Mars-Jones takes exception to the pairing of Julian and Rose: "For once, the author's desire for a plot-twist takes precedence over

THE ACCIDENTAL TOURIST

truth to character: Rose has been portrayed with such dry sexlessness that when she mentions Julian's romantic interest in her the reader is cued to diagnose virgin dementia. Much more satisfying is the moment some time after their marriage when Rose moves back with her b[r]others, and then Julian moves in too . . . Julian's obsession has always been with the household as much as with Rose" (1096).

11. Macon sounds more than a little like Anne Tyler herself: "I like routine and rituals and I hate leaving home; I have a sense of digging my heels in. I refuse to drive on freeways. I dread our annual vacation. Yet I'm continually prepared for travel: it is physically impossible for me to buy any necessity without buying a travel-sized version as well. I have a little toilet kit, with soap and a nightgown, forever packed and ready to go" ("Still Just Writing," in Janet Sternburg, ed., *The Writer on Her Work* [New York: Norton, 1980]: 15).

12. Lee Lescaze terms Edward "the most winning Welsh corgi in American fiction" ("Throwing Caution to the Whim," *The Wall Street Journal* 206 [16 September 1985]: 22). But notes Anne R. Zahlan, "Tyler's Edward, probably the book's most captivating character, is . . . more than a scene-stealer; he is the id in canine form. It is Edward who expresses the rage and confusion that Macon so carefully represses" (500). Edward's special status in the novel would help explain what Larry McMurtry regards as a major technical problem: "the unaccountable neglect of Edward . . . in the last third of the book" (36). If indeed Edward is the emblem of his owner's fear, frustration, and anger, then his disappearance from the novel confirms Macon's psychological recovery.

13. Joseph Mathewson, for example, writes that Tyler has done "such a bang-up job of making me believe in the fixed qualities of her people that I had a few bad moments when some of the characters did begin to change." When Macon was kindly to Mrs. Bunn, "I must confess to wishing that he still had his nose in *Miss MacIntosh*" (14).

14. In 1989, Tyler explained that she originally had not ended *The Accidental Tourist* in its present form: "I wrote an entire final chapter in which Macon stayed with Sarah and then realized I couldn't do

it—not only because it spoiled the dramatic line of the plot but also because it meant abandoning Alexander." She sees the present ending as a positive one: "I see Macon and Muriel in an edgy, incongruous but ultimately workable marriage, Macon forever frustrated by Muriel's behavior and yet more flexible than his old self. Alexander turns out *wonderfully*. (By that I mean: happy)" (Interview with AHP).

15. Lee Lescaze argues that Tyler's "plot is conventional and telegraphs its twists in advance," while occasionally it "totters toward sentimentality" (22). Adam Mars-Jones bemoans its "patches of cuteness or banality," while admitting that "they are always surrounded by passages that treat the same material with confident freshness" (1096). The anonymous commentator in *The Antioch Review* 44 (Spring 1986) called it "a standard soap-opera plot" (249). Even Updike admits that Muriel's regenerative impact on Macon is "predictable" (108).

CHAPTER TEN

Breathing Lessons

One might say that Anne Tyler's eleventh novel, *Breathing Lessons* (1988), had a mixed critical response. On the one hand, David Klinghoffer of *The National Review* spoke for many in wondering "what kind of contractual obligations the talented Miss Tyler had that convinced her to dig this one out of her manuscript drawer."[1] On the other hand, it received the Pulitzer Prize for Fiction. Of course, there are no guarantees that this coveted award always goes to a writer's finest novel (witness Willa Cather's *One of Ours* [1923] and William Faulkner's *A Fable* [1955]); but the Pulitzer does tend to go to writers who, by virtue of past literary achievements, political conditions, and/or social climate, are seen as having arrived—and after ten novels, most of them good or excellent, Tyler had indeed seemed to have established a firm and respected niche in contemporary American letters by the time the Pulitzers were awarded in late March 1989. Thus the quality of her eleventh novel would be, in the minds of the Pulitzer committee members, something of a moot point in their desire to honor Tyler's considerable achievements over the previous quarter of a century; and in fact one can say in all fairness that *Breathing Lessons* is not Tyler's finest novel. It is, as most critics contend, a "slenderer" story than such efforts as *The Accidental Tourist* and *Dinner at the Homesick Restaurant*[2]—slenderer not just in time frame (about twelve hours) or characterization (two rather "flat" protagonists), but in theme and technique. Many contemporary reviewers seemed dismayed by the seeming harping on TV-movie-level concerns about middle age and the empty nest syndrome. Others were disappointed that there seemed to be nothing new in Tyler's latest effort: "This is a world that by now we know too well. Even loyal fans and readers deserve to be surprised."[3] Still others were put off by the apparent failure of the novel's title and central metaphor, "breathing lessons," to enrich and inform the story.[4] Not since *Morgan's Passing* had a Tyler novel been so subjected to accusations of lack of authorial control: Klinghoffer bemoans the fact that "Miss Tyler gives Maggie three pages to maneuver her Chevy out of a tough parking space," while Robert McPhillips characterizes the novel after the Morans' expulsion from the funeral reception as a "two-hundred-page denouement."[5] Perhaps most damning of all, many critics found the novel seriously compromised by inappropriate humor. Robert Towers spoke for many in maintaining that after the funeral reception, "Tyler had allowed her novel to slip into whimsy and slapstick,"[6] especially in regard to Maggie herself—a character whose meddling and antics seemed only to generate rancor in the critical community. Maggie's "Lucy Ricardo quality," observes Marita Golden, "undermines our empathy";[7] and with that lost, so is the impact of much of the novel. Many of these criticisms are richly justified, but this does not gainsay that Tyler raises some vital questions in *Breathing Lessons.* The most important are two related issues around which the novel revolves: What are the components of a healthy, lasting marriage? And how can one deal constructively with the inevitable passage of time?

Tyler explores the first issue by focusing on three different marriages. One, that of young Jesse Moran and Fiona Stuckey, failed at the outset. The other two involve middle-aged contemporaries: Max and Serena Gill, and Ira and Maggie Moran. Each relationship is unique, having been based on particular needs and expectations, and each succeeds or fails as the result of different internal and external pressures. Viewed collectively, they offer a sensitive and complex portrait of what is wrong—and right—with marriage as an institution in late twentieth-century America.

The marriage of Jesse and Fiona is arguably the saddest of the three, as it was based largely upon misunderstanding. Fiona Stuckey seems to have fallen in love not with Jesse Moran, but rather with his persona as the handsome lead singer of a hard-rock band. A determined groupie, she pursues him, not realizing until after their daughter Leroy is born that he is nothing more than the usually-unpaid singer of a failed local band, and that his spurts of enthusiasm for anything else—be it the pursuit of a career in computers or the construction of baby furniture—is well-meant but short-lived. Even his marriage is this way: armed with his Dr. Spock baby book, Jesse is momentarily enthralled with the advantages of breast-feeding and the progress of cervical dilation during labor; but once the child is born—a daughter instead of the son he assumed he would have—much of Jesse's interest in marriage and fatherhood has ended. By the time of the cataclysmic blow-up during a birthday picnic at Pimlico race track, Jesse has reverted to his earlier egocentric ways, associating with other women, drinking too much beer, and leaving baby Leroy in the sole care of Fiona, who realizes with a shock that she had agreed to forego the abortion and to marry him only because she thought he was a genuinely domestic type. "I married you for [the] cradle" he supposedly was building for their unborn child (278, 269), when in fact he had never even begun the project. It does not occur to Fiona that the qualities she admired in his rock-star persona (cool, aloof, sexually dangerous) are precisely those which would render him poor material as a husband and father. And yet, these are domestic roles that Jesse would have liked to pursue, but could not.

In large measure, Tyler attributes Jesse's difficulties to the times in which he lives—times which dictate that

BREATHING LESSONS

the way to happiness is self-indulgence. And not since
A Slipping-Down Life has Tyler argued so forcefully that
the medium carrying that message is popular music.
With a weak singing voice, Jesse essentially speaks his
lyrics, relying heavily on his black denim outfits to flesh
out his rock-star persona—as, indeed, did Drumstrings
Casey. And the lyrics that he speaks and listens to dis-
tort romance into a fundamentally selfish emotion. As
his mother Maggie points out, the anthem of Jesse's
generation is "Help Me Make It Through the Night."
No wonder Jesse feels no particular qualms over sleeping with Fiona in his own bedroom at home *sans* birth
control, no guilt over his mother discovering the affair,
no misgivings over reverting to his irresponsible bache-
lor ways once his child is born. Immediate self-gratifica-
tion is all he knows.

And yet at least part of the blame rests squarely
with his mother. Having been raised in a household
that rendered self-denial a fine art, and that was so
filled with "educational" classical music that she came
thoroughly to despise it, Maggie made a conscious decision to raise her own children differently, declining
even to correct their mistakes in grammar. She preferred "to hear what it was they had to say and let the
grammar take care of itself. Not that it had done so, at
least not in Jesse's case" (270, *261*). But the distress of
this realization nevertheless fails to prevent her from
encouraging her son in his doomed career as a rock star,
as she persistently calls him a "musician" while her hus-

band Ira "had never thought of Jesse as a musician; he'd thought of him as a high-school dropout in need of permanent employment" (160, *155*). Like Jesse, Maggie meant well; like him, she ultimately ended up doing more harm than good, unwittingly instilling standards and expectations in her son that could bode only ill for any kind of permanent adult relationship.

To her credit, Maggie does recognize that there is a spark of something serious between Jesse and Fiona, some inkling of a desire to forge a happy home: "They've always loved each other; they never stopped; it's just that they can't, oh, connect, somehow" (11, *10*). The failure to connect which is such a powerful recurring element in Tyler's novels is perhaps most dramatic in *Breathing Lessons*, in which Jesse and Fiona can literally connect in just one way—genitally. Beyond that, they cannot even talk to one another. Maggie serves as a frantic go-between who falsely attributes statements and motives to each: engineering a conciliatory dinner by telephone, she reports to Fiona that Jesse had said to her, "I'll be right there after work, Ma! You can count on me! . . . Goddamn! I wouldn't miss it for the world!" (223, *215*). But the spark can be ignited only by themselves, and with just the doubtful nurturing and maneuvering of Maggie and the slatternly Mrs. Stuckey behind them, Jesse and Fiona are incapable of staying together in a strong, mutually supportive marriage.

In dramatic contrast, the marriage of Serena and Max Gill, whose untimely death from cancer is the basis of the funeral trip around which the novel is constructed, proved strong and happy despite unpromising beginnings. Serena Palermo would hardly have seemed like the type to have a good marriage. The illegitimate daughter of a woman fond of "bright-red, skin-tight toreador pants" (65, *63*), Serena was a study in the non-traditional, eating sardines for school lunch in the third grade and even getting her ears pierced in conservative, sanitary post-World War II America. But she had decided at an early age that she would have an adult life counter to the one experienced by her mother. As she explained to best friend Maggie while surreptitiously studying the mansion of her biological father (cf. Maggie's own "spy trips" to watch Fiona and Leroy many years later), Serena refused to be "love's victim" (72, *69*), and she wasn't. She went for "not the dark Lotharios you would expect," but "the plaid-shirt boys, the gym-sneaker boys"—"sunny innocents like Max" (66, *63*). And to keep Max Gill, whose parents had sent him to Chapel Hill with the expressed purpose of exposing him to more suitable potential wives, Serena did the one thing available to her: she refused to engage in premarital sex. Responding not to the dictates of her conservative era but to her own sense of the need for emotional stability, she does what she must to attract and keep him, and she continues her policy of working at the relationship even after the wedding. In terms of his career, Max had proved to be "a bit of a failure," but Serena was willing to "carry" him (71, *68*), to take up the slack left by her husband. But at the same time, she never lost her sense of individuality within the marriage: she and Max continued to call each other by their surnames, and "it had made the two of them look more amiable than other married couples. They'd seemed like easygoing buddies, unaware of that dark, helpless, angry, confined feeling that Maggie's own marriage descended to from time to time" (71, *68*). Though she may not have been passionately in love with Max when she married him—she had decided it was "just *time* to marry" (113, *109*)—and though she was vocal in her disgust over the sedentary lifestyle that had led to his early death, Serena nonetheless had experienced, as her name suggests, a deliberately forged degree of serenity in her life. Theirs was a good relationship, as confirmed by her desire to replay their wedding, solos and all, at his funeral service. Tyler creates a final impression of Serena as someone who has had the best kind of marriage: one that leaves her strong enough to survive alone after her mate's death.

The marriage of Serena's contemporaries Ira and Maggie Moran is more problematical. Like Jesse and Fiona's, it originated in a misunderstanding. Having been told incorrectly at choir practice that Ira Moran, a boy two years older than she, had been killed in an accident at boot camp, Maggie Daley had sent his father a formal note of condolence in which she expressed feelings that she didn't realize she harbored: *"I thought Ira was the most wonderful person I've ever met. There was*

something special about him" (103, *99*). These strong feelings seem to have been confirmed in Ira's response to
her mistake. Refusing to ridicule her as his father does
(Sam Moran henceforth calls her "Madam" [169, *163*]),
Ira is genuinely touched by this woman who seems so
supportive of his desire to become a physician—and
who is a means of denying his father's hold over his life.
When "weak hearted" Sam tells Maggie that Ira
"wouldn't dare" refuse to support himself and Ira's two
spinster sisters, Ira suddenly declares "I'm marrying
her anyhow" (119, *115*)—an arrangement which Maggie
allows herself to be swept into in part on the strength
of Serena's conviction that Ira, darkly handsome thanks
to a few drops of Cherokee blood, is "a mystery" (14).
In singing "Love is a Many Splendored Thing" as a duet
at Serena's wedding, Ira and Maggie seem to have confirmed the complex emotions underlying their own relationship.

Married for twenty-eight years at the time *Breathing
Lessons* opens, Ira and Maggie are surely not enjoying
the kind of relationship that their 1950s' courtship had
trumpeted: they are well aware of the justice of Serena's
warning that marriage is not "a Rock Hudson-Doris Day
movie" (57, *54*). After all, Ira's father had won out: the
young man's agreement to take over Sam's picture-
framing business on a temporary basis had turned into
a lifelong commitment to support his father and his sisters Junie and Dorrie. At the same time, he had to support Maggie and their own children, Jesse and Daisy.

One cannot blame him for resenting Jesse—or, as Maggie surmises, for being envious of him. With the opportunity to do as he wishes and no pressure to assume responsibility for his own daughter, parents, or sister, Jesse is enjoying the kind of life that was denied Ira. More subtly, Jesse is acting, albeit inappropriately, on a conviction that haunts his father: that to "die unknown" is a horrible fate. "No compromises for Jesse Moran, no, sir. No modifications, no lowering of sights for Jesse" (166, *161*)—the implication being that Ira had essentially sold out his dreams rather than acquiesced to responsibility. And much of that responsibility revolved around his two children, whom Ira regards as "outsiders" who interrupt his and Maggie's "most private moments, wedging between the two of them" (153–54, *148*).

For the fact is that Ira loves Maggie dearly, and one of the sorriest aspects of their marriage is that she does not comprehend this. In one of their many arguments throughout the novel, Maggie accuses him of believing she is "a whifflehead" (35, *33*); and although there is ample evidence to support this impression—the fender-bender with the Pepsi truck; the wild ride in the nursing home laundry cart; the inadvertent murder of her kitten Thistledown, tumbled to death in the family clothes dryer—there really is nothing to suggest that Ira feels his wife is a mindless clown. To be sure, he is annoyed that she tells her personal woes to total strangers, and he is understandably miffed that she leaves the road map at home. But in general he is commendably patient and even-tempered, expressing his feelings eloquently, if indirectly, through the tunes that he whistles. And what little anger he does feel is directed not at Maggie, but at the possible damage to others that her meddling may cause, or at the needless distress she causes herself by worrying. And much as Ira loves Maggie, she loves him: "In love with her own husband! The convenience of it pleased her—like finding right in her pantry all the fixings she needed for a new recipe" (123, *118*).

Even Ira's fondness for playing solitaire should not be seen as a negative comment on their marriage. It is, of course, a game to be played by one person alone, and Ira tells Maggie bluntly to "butt out" (52, *49*) when she tries to interfere. And yet the solitariness of this pursuit is fundamentally healthy: Ira is preserving his individuality and distance in the marriage, in the same way that Serena and Max preserved theirs by using each other's surname. Maggie does essentially the same thing by insisting on continuing to work as a geriatric nursing assistant at the Silver Threads Nursing Home, a job which she took only because it was a means of defying her mother, an English teacher who insisted she attend Goucher College, but more importantly because it made her feel "valuable and competent" (95, *91*). Though her salary is meager, Maggie derives a strong sense of personal identity and emotional strength by helping the elderly: like Ira's card game, it is an activity that she must pursue alone. More subtly, the solitaire game serves as an emblem of marriage itself. At the beginning of the game, the moves are easy, the possibilities seemingly endless. "I ought to have an amateur work this part," declares Ira, "the way the old masters had their students fill in the backgrounds of their paintings" (51–52, 49). But as the game progresses, "his choices were narrower and he had to show real skill and judgment" (338, 327). A game unusual in that it allows for degrees of success rather than simple winning or losing, solitaire is an apt symbol of the Morans' marriage. There are occasional mistakes or rough spots: Maggie, for example, engaged in a "reverse courtship" with old Mr. Gabriel (40, 39) and experienced sexual dreams involving a neighbor man, while Ira stonily declined to sing a duet with Maggie at Max's funeral. But at this stage of the marital game, nothing either spouse does will cause total loss. As Ira realizes, their relationship is "as steady as a tree; not even he could tell how wide and deep the roots went" (163, 157). Their "skill and judgment" will see them through, as they travel along life's highway in an appropriately dinged, dented, but still-running Dodge, sometimes silent, and sometimes harmonizing to "On the Road Again."[8]

And the Morans are fortunate that their marriage is so solid, for it is their only refuge against the ravages of time itself. As is evident from her earlier novels, in particular *The Clock Winder* and *Morgan's Passing*, Tyler is a writer deeply concerned with the joys and difficulties of reaching certain stages of life: adolescence, young adulthood, middle age, old age. Her novels move more or less through chronological stages in keeping with those experienced by Tyler herself, from the young adulthood of *If Morning Ever Comes,* to the encroaching middle age of *Earthly Possessions,* to the full-blown middle years of *Morgan's Passing.* But not until *Breathing Lessons* has Tyler focused so clearly on the issue of time as an abstraction and the impact of its passing on individual lives.

The funeral-cum-class-reunion and the reception scenes which most commentators regard as the highlight of the novel insist almost too much on the self-evident truth that seeing old friends after nearly thirty years can be an unsettling experience.[9] The members of the Class of '56 who participate in Max's memorial service are not, Maggie is stunned to realize, "still fretting over Prom Night" (90, *87*). They have aged at the same time that she has, though they make desperate efforts to appear forever young. The Barley twins, for example, still "wore their yellow hair in the short, curly, caplike style they'd favored in high school," but "the backs of their necks were scrawny as chicken necks and their fussy pink ruffles gave them a Minnie Pearl look" (69, *66*). Likewise, Sugar Tilghman has skin that certainly appears "smooth and taut beneath [her] veil," like an onion in nylon netting; but without the veil, Sugar "was older-looking than Maggie had first realized" (62, *59*). To underscore dramatically the changes from youth to middle age, Tyler depicts soloist Durwood Clegg "shift[ing] back and forth like those trick portraits that change expression according to where you're standing: the old lady-killer Durwood meaningfully lingering on *darling, you're all that I'm living for . . .* , but then the present-day, shabby Durwood searching for the next stanza on [his paper], which he held at arm's length, with his forehead wrinkled, as he tried to make out the words" (73–74, *70–71*). The paper on which he has jotted down the lyrics is a grocery store coupon for Affinity shampoo, which allegedly *"Brings back the fullness that time has taken away"* (307, *297*).

The impulse to restore youth, to cling to what's left, or to pretend it is still viable is an idea that can wear thin quickly, especially when used as the linchpin of an entire novel. So Tyler ranges beyond the self-evident tragicomedy of the shock of middle age by examining *why*, beyond aesthetic considerations, it is such a shock. For one thing, it signifies the loss of youthful promises and dreams. These can be fairly mundane, like Serena and Maggie's promises that "we wouldn't mince when we walked barefoot": "We promised we wouldn't wash the dishes right after supper," either, "because that would take us away from our husbands; remember that? How long since you saved the dishes till morning so you could be with Max? How long since Max even noticed that you didn't?" (23–24, *23*). Even more unsettling are the dashed dreams of Ira Moran, who still chafes at his failure to realize his youthful ambition to become a physician: "He was fifty years old and had never accomplished one single act of consequence. Once he had planned to find a cure for some major disease and now he was framing petit point instead" (129, *125*). What makes Ira's situation particularly painful is that he had never actively decided to abandon his dream of medical school. It had slipped away, as he initially postponed college for a summer to look after the frame-shop, and then as the season stretched into years. The injustice of this loss leaves Ira often feeling "the most crushing kind of tiredness" (154, *149*) and acute anger, especially over the prospect of wastefulness in any form. His situation is emblematized by a disastrous outing to Baltimore's Harborplace development. Trying to please his family, Ira finds himself in a literal fog, trying to deal with his hyperventilating father, his agoraphobic sister Junie, and his physically and mentally handicapped sister Dorrie: "Was it any wonder he was so sensitive to waste? He had given up the only serious dream he'd ever had. You can't get more wasteful than that" (172, *166*). Though later he will realize that the "true waste" is "his failure to notice how he loved" his father and sisters (181, *175*), the fact remains that after nearly thirty years of marriage Ira still bemoans the loss of his lifelong dreams of a career in medicine. Time clearly does not heal all.

Indeed, time has the unique capacity to destroy. Max Gill, whose funeral precipitates the novel's action, is not yet fifty years old when he dies of cancer, but towards the end of his life he had seemed a very old

UNDERSTANDING ANNE TYLER

man. Serena had in fact not realized how seriously her husband was ill until she looked at him one April morning and thought, "My Lord, he's so old! His whole face is different" (54, *51*)). Soon he began to wander off from home in his premature senility, and not long after he died. Max's situation is a symbol for Maggie of a phenomenon she herself is experiencing: the feeling that time is out of her control, that it is accelerating—and that as a result, years have slipped by without her realizing it. This frightening prospect causes her to engage in activities and to make statements which, taken out of context, do indeed make her look ridiculous. She is visibly distressed that she cannot remember the term "car pool," for "it seems like just last week that Jesse had a game or hockey camp, Daisy had a Brownie meeting" to which they had to be driven (9). She is likewise upset to realize that her father-in-law's great-grandfather had been born in the 1700s. And she becomes frantic when she feels that her car's odometer is out of synchronization with the highway's mileage test. "Slow down!" she commands Ira. "We're losing! We're too far ahead" (25)—a paradox which she finds as unsettling as the sudden absence of "the steady, faithful whir" of the disconnected dehumidifier (186, *180*).

But in fact the passage of time, like the tripping of the odometer, is orderly and regular; and much of the impact of *Breathing Lessons* is derived from Maggie's efforts to recognize and accept not only that time is not accelerated as one ages, but that time the destroyer does

BREATHING LESSONS

not destroy all—and that what is lost is probably better off that way. In their determination to restore youth despite gray hair and the need for reading glasses, the participants in Max's memorial service are forgetting that in many ways they have changed for the better over time. "Sugar," after all, is now a more mature "Elizabeth." Further, they have left behind youthful self-images that were far less appealing than their memories would suggest. Watching the home movie of Serena and Max's wedding after the funeral, most of the participants are appalled at what they looked like twenty-nine years earlier. They yearn, significantly, to "fast-forward" the film (92, *89*). And since the movie has no sound track, they are spared other harsh realities that they have selectively repressed, including Serena's shouting at her new husband over his failure during their march back up the aisle to keep time with the recessional music. The sense of being out of synchronization thus is hardly a problem unique to middle age, and the past is sometimes better left there.

By the same token, much of the good of the past is retained over time. The "silver bell" of Maggie's voice, now "nearly half a century old," does indeed crack (61, *58*), but it is still serviceable. And though Maggie and her husband seem somehow to have turned into the figures of a childhood picture entitled "Old Folks at Home" (136, *132*), Ira still occasionally appears "like a bashful young boy" (195, *189*). For Tyler would argue that life and time are best seen not as a continuum with the past faded or lost, but as a series of layers. Ideas and feelings accumulate over time, like the clothes in Fiona's drawer: "It was like the layers in an archaeological dig. Maggie had the fleeting fantasy that if she delved farther she would find cheerleader sweaters, then grade-school pinafores, then Fiona's baby clothes" (284–85, 275). Layering is one of Tyler's most persistent motifs, seen as early as the leaves piled outside the Hawkeses' door in *If Morning Ever Comes*. But Tyler expands it further in *Breathing Lessons* by introducing what at first blush sounds like a juvenile concept: the heavenly gunnysack.

It was an idea first proposed to Maggie by an elderly patient in the nursing home. When he died, he believed, St. Peter would hand him in his own personal gunnysack all that he had lost in his lifetime, including "the little red sweater his mother had knit him just before she died, that he had left on a bus in fourth grade and missed with all his heart ever since" (327, 316). Maggie embraces the concept, believing that her heavenly gunnysack will contain all her "misplaced compacts, single earrings, and [lost] umbrellas" (327, 316). But as she muses further, the gunnysack expands to include her beloved plastic necklace, lost by Daisy while jumping rope one summer evening: "Definitely that would be in the gunnysack. And the summer evening as well, why not—the children smelling of sweat and fireflies, the warm porch floorboards sticking slightly to your chair rockers, the voices ringing from the alley"

(329, *318*). Like the lyrics of the 50s' popular tunes that can be recalled if one tries hard enough, nothing good from the past is ever fully lost: it is nestled somewhere in a layer of the gunnysack of the psyche. Armed with that consoling thought, Maggie can face the future and personal change with equanimity. As the novel closes, she prepares to deal directly with a major life change: driving Daisy to college, and looking forward to spending the rest of her life with just Ira in the house.

The "lessons" learned in the course of the novel thus have little to do with the proper breathing required for childbirth, and much to do with day-to-day existence. There are some things for which no one else can prepare us: "you're given all these lessons for the unimportant things—piano-playing, typing. You're given years and years of lessons in how to balance equations, which Lord knows you will never have to do in normal life. But how about parenthood? Or marriage . . . Before you can drive a car you need a state-approved course of instruction, but driving a car is nothing, nothing, compared to living day in and day out with a husband and raising up a new human being" (188, *182*). Maggie Moran has had to learn for herself, through painful experience and observation, how to place marriage, time, and life itself into a perspective that would enable her to continue down a not always smooth road. Like the legion of Tyler characters before her, Maggie Moran endures.

UNDERSTANDING ANNE TYLER

Notes

1. David Klinghoffer, "Ordinary People," *The National Review* 40 (30 December 1988): 49.

2. Observes Lee Lescaze, "it is a slenderer story [than *Dinner at the Homesick Restaurant*], but readers of Maggie and Ira's age, who have made compromises of their own and fought off their own attacks of despair, will find the novel particularly moving" ("Mid-Life Ups and Downs," *The Wall Street Journal* 212 [6 September 1988]: 28). Edward Hoagland felt that it offers "a slightly thinner mixture" than *The Accidental Tourist:* "It lacks a *Muriel*, for one thing" ("About Maggie, Who Tried Too Hard," *New York Times Book Review* [11 September 1988]: 44). Likewise comparing *Breathing Lessons* unfavorably to *The Accidental Tourist,* Robert Towers felt it was "less substantial, more susceptible to the tendencies to whimsicality and even cuteness that sometimes affect [Tyler's] work" ("Roughing It," *The New York Review of Books* 35 [10 November 1988]: 40).

3. Marita Golden, "New Wives' Tales," *Ms.* 17 (September 1988): 86.

4. Robert McPhillips observes that Tyler usually relies on a "central organizing metaphor," the "most successful" of which is Ezra's Homesick Restaurant. The idea of "breathing lessons" is "far less resonant" as a controlling metaphor "than those in her best novels" ("The Baltimore Chop," *The Nation* 247 [7 November 1988]: 464, 466).

5. Klinghoffer 48; McPhillips 465.

6. Towers 41. Hoagland felt that Tyler had introduced elements of "unfunny slapstick, as if in an effort to corral extra readers. I don't believe Ms. Tyler should think she needs to tinker with her popularity" (44).

7. Golden 86. Klinghoffer termed Maggie "pathetic" (49), while Towers felt that "Maggie sometimes seems too broad in relation to the much subtler handling of the other characters—she is too awkward, too silly, to carry the burden that has been assigned to her. The sentimentality in the conception of her character becomes an irritation"

(41). One of the few critics to defend Maggie is Wallace Stegner, who feels that her "essential goodness and capacity for affection make us want to comfort rather than kick her" ("The Meddler's Progress," *Washington Post Book World* 18 [4 September 1988]: 1).

8. McPhillips observes that "this novel's journey presents a vision of marriage as a very rocky road" (464). And although the Morans end up literally where they began, at home in Baltimore, it is important to remember that emotionally they (and especially Maggie) have made considerable progress in the course of the day's travels. The apparent circularity of their spatial movements thus should not be seen as indicative of hopelessness or stasis.

9. Even Tyler's most censorious commentators grant that the funeral and reception scenes are the strongest in the book. Golden, for example, feels that they set "off sparks that make the story crackle with humor and wisdom" (86). Towers, however, feels that these scenes are "simply preposterous" (41).

BIBLIOGRAPHY

Books by Anne Tyler

If Morning Ever Comes. New York: Knopf, 1964; London: Chatto & Windus, 1965.

The Tin Can Tree. New York: Knopf, 1965; London: Macmillan, 1966.

A Slipping-Down Life. New York: Knopf, 1970; London; Severn House, 1983.

The Clock Winder. New York: Knopf, 1972; London: Chatto & Windus, 1973.

Celestial Navigation. New York: Knopf, 1974; London: Chatto & Windus, 1975.

Searching for Caleb. New York: Knopf, 1976; London: Chatto & Windus, 1976.

Earthly Possessions. New York: Knopf, 1977; London: Chatto & Windus, 1977.

Morgan's Passing. New York: Knopf, 1980; London: Chatto & Windus, 1980.

Dinner at the Homesick Restaurant. New York: Knopf, 1982; London: Chatto & Windus, 1982.

The Accidental Tourist. New York: Knopf, 1985; London: Chatto & Windus, 1985.

Breathing Lessons. New York: Knopf, 1988; London: Chatto & Windus, 1989.

Secondary Bibliography
Bibliographies and Checklists

Gardiner, Elaine and Catherine Rainwater. "A Bibliography of Writings by Anne Tyler." Appendix to essay by Mary F. Robertson in Catherine Rainwater and William J. Scheick, eds. *Contemporary American Women Writers: Narrative Strategies.* Lexington: UP of Kentucky, 1985: 142–52. Includes comprehensive list of short stories, articles, and book reviews by Tyler.

Nesanovich, Stella. "An Anne Tyler Checklist, 1959–1980." *Bulletin of Bibliography* 38 (April–June 1981): 53–64. Primary and secondary bibliography.

Interviews, Personal Statements, and Biographical Sketches

Brown, Laurie L. "Interviews with Seven Contemporary Writers." *Southern Quarterly* 21 (Summer 1983): 3–22. Focuses on Tyler's life and writing habits.

Cook, Bruce. "New Faces in Faulkner Country." *Saturday Review* 3 (4 September 1976): 39–41. Includes commentary by Tyler on the contemporary literary scene in the South and her place within it.

———. "A Writer—During School Hours." *Detroit News* (6 April 1980), Sec. E: 1, 3. Tyler discusses the challenges of juggling a writing career with raising a family, with special attention paid to *Morgan's Passing*.

English, Sarah. "Anne Tyler." In *The Dictionary of Literary Biography Yearbook: 1982*. Detroit: Gale Research, 1983: 193–94. Includes a wide-ranging interview.

Lamb, Wendy. "An Interview with Anne Tyler." *Iowa Journal of Literary Studies* 3 (1981): 59–64. An important, provocative interview that touches upon such matters as writing habits, book critics, and Tyler's own feelings about her work.

Lueloff, Jorie. "Authoress Explains Why Women Dominate in South." *[Baton Rouge] Morning Advocate* (8 February 1965), Sec. A: 11. A frank, chatty interview conducted when Tyler was still living in Montreal. Tyler addresses in particular the status of women writers in the South.

Michaels, Marguerite. "Anne Tyler, Writer 8:05 to 3:30." *New York Times Book Review* (8 May 1977): 13, 42–43. Focuses on

BIBLIOGRAPHY

the difficulties Tyler faced in the mid-1970s as a professional writer who also was a full-time housewife and mother.

Ridley, Clifford A. "Anne Tyler: A Sense of Reticence Balanced by 'Oh, Well, Why Not?'" *National Observer* 11 (22 July 1972): 23. Includes Tyler's appraisals of her changing attitude towards her life and work, with special reference to *The Clock Winder*.

Tyler, Anne. "Because I Want More Than One Life." *Washington Post* (15 August 1976), Sec. G: 1, 7. Account of the rituals and routines Tyler utilizes in the act of writing.

————. "Olives Out of a Bottle." *[Duke University] Archive* 87 (Spring 1975): 70–79. The partial transcript of a panel discussion including Tyler.

————. "Still Just Writing." In Janet Sternburg, ed. *The Writer on Her Work.* New York: Norton, 1980: 3–16. A personal meditation on the difficulties of maintaining a serious writing career while also being a housewife and mother.

Critical Essays

Betts, Doris. "The Fiction of Anne Tyler." *Southern Quarterly* 21 (Summer 1983): 23–37. Argues that Tyler's first "nine novels over seventeen years trace her own accommodation of the methods of the short story, methods geared to change and revelation, until they become adapted to her more novelistic conclusions about a Reality which changes very little . . ."

Binding, Paul. "Anne Tyler." In *Separate Country: A Literary Journey through the American South.* New York & London: Paddington Press, 1979: 198–209. A personal meditation on Tyler, her novels, and the South.

Bowers, Bradley R. "Anne Tyler's Insiders." *Mississippi Quar-*

BIBLIOGRAPHY

terly 42 (Winter 1988–89): 47–56. Argues that in her novels Tyler creates a unique perspective "which includes not only certain family members but the narrator and the reader as well, all of whom form [a] group of insiders."

Brooks, Mary Ellen. "Anne Tyler." In *The Dictionary of Literary Biography*. Vol. 6: *American Novelists Since World War II*. Detroit: Gale Research, 1980: 336–45. General overview of Tyler's career up through *Morgan's Passing*.

Elkins, Mary J. "*Dinner at the Homesick Restaurant:* Anne Tyler and the Faulkner Connection." *Atlantis* 10 (Spring 1985): 93–105. A somewhat strained attempt to trace the parallels between *Dinner* and Faulkner's *As I Lay Dying*.

Gibson, Mary Ellis. "Family as Fate: The Novels of Anne Tyler." *Southern Literary Journal* 16 (Fall 1983): 47–58. Discusses *Dinner at the Homesick Restaurant* within Classical and existential frameworks.

Gullette, Margaret Morganroth. "The Tears (and Joys) Are in the Things: Adulthood in Anne Tyler's Novels." *New England Review and Bread Loaf Quarterly* 7 (Spring 1985): 323–34. Provocative analysis which traces the importance of attitudes towards "things" in the delineation of maturity level in Tyler's fiction.

Jones, Anne G. "Home at Last, and Homesick Again: The Ten Novels of Anne Tyler." *The Hollins Critic* 23 (April 1986): 1–14. Excellent overview of Tyler's achievement in her first ten novels.

Miller, Laura. "Woman as Hostage: Escape to Freedom or Journey into Bondage?" In Malcolm Hayward, ed. *Proceedings of the Second Annual Conference of EAPSCU* [English Association of the Pennsylvania State Colleges and Univer-

BIBLIOGRAPHY

sities] (1983): 49–52. Attempts to trace parallels between *Earthly Possessions* and Doris Betts's 1981 novel *Heading West*. Of little value.

Nesanovich, Stella. "The Individual in the Family: Anne Tyler's *Searching for Caleb* and *Earthly Possessions*." *Southern Review* 14 (January 1978): 170–76. Focuses on these two novels to explore the problematic relationships between individual needs and familial expectations in Tyler's world view.

Robertson, Mary F. "Anne Tyler: Medusa Points and Contact Points." In Catherine Rainwater and William J. Scheick, eds. *Contemporary American Women Writers: Narrative Strategies*. Lexington: UP of Kentucky, 1985: 119–52. Traces the patterns of connection and misconnection ("Medusa points") in Tyler's novels. A substantial, intelligent study, marred by the complexities of the Medusa point paradigm.

Shelton, Frank W. "The Necessary Balance: Distance and Sympathy in the Novels of Anne Tyler." *Southern Review* 20 (Autumn 1984): 851–60. Argues that the "central issue" in Tyler's novels is the degree to which the individual can "retain the distance from others necessary for a modicum of personal freedom" while achieving "enough closeness to others to share necessary human warmth and sympathy."

Updike, John. "Family Ways." *The New Yorker* 52 (29 March 1976): 110–12. This thoughtful review of *Searching for Caleb* was instrumental in introducing Tyler to a wide reading public.

———. "Leaving Home." *The New Yorker* 61 (28 October 1985): 106–08, 110–12. Despite some reservations, Updike offers a generally favorable review of *The Accidental Tourist*.

———. "Loosened Roots." *The New Yorker* 53 (6 June 1977): 130, 133–34. Favorable review of *Earthly Possessions*.

259

BIBLIOGRAPHY

———. "On Such a Beautiful Green Little Planet." *The New Yorker* 58 (5 April 1982): 193–97. Insightful, enthusiastic review of *Dinner at the Homesick Restaurant*.

Zahlan, Anne R. "Anne Tyler." In Joseph M. Flora and Robert Bain, eds. *Fifty Southern Writers After 1900: A Bio-Bibliographical Sourcebook*. Westport, Connecticut: Greenwood Press, 1987: 491–504. Solid biocritical essay, complete through *The Accidental Tourist*.

INDEX

Page numbers in bold type denote extended discussion of Tyler's works.

INDEX

INDEX

INDEX

INDEX

INDEX